IN T⬛⬛E

BY LISA ⬛⬛ON

DRAMATISTS
PLAY SERVICE
INC.

IN THE WAKE
Copyright © 2012, Lisa Kron

All Rights Reserved

SPECIAL NOTE

IN THE WAKE was commissioned by Center Theater Group.

The world premiere was co-produced by
Center Theater Group at the Kirk Douglas Theatre in Los Angeles, CA in March 2010
and Berkeley Repertory Theatre at the Roda Theatre in Berkeley, CA in May 2010.

The New York premiere of IN THE WAKE was produced
by the Public Theater in October 2010

Oskar Eustis	Andrew D. Hamingson
Artistic Director	Executive Director

IN THE WAKE was developed, in part, with the assistance
of the Sundance Institute Theater Program.

ACKNOWLEDGMENTS

My heartfelt thanks to the following people: Kathy Bailey, Michael Kavanagh, Joann Kingsley, Ben Kron, and especially Loretta Mears for conversations that helped inspire and shape this play; John Dias, Oskar Eustis, Adam Greenfield, Mandy Hackett, Madeleine Oldham, Pier Carlo Talenti, and Tony Taccone for their dramaturgical support and insight; and finally, and most especially to my cherished collaborator Leigh Silverman for brilliant guidance every step of the way.

IN THE WAKE received its New York premiere at the Public Theater in New York City on November 1, 2010. It was directed by Leigh Silverman; the set design was by David Korins; the costume design was by Susan Hilferty; the lighting and projection design were by Alexander V. Nichols; the sound design was by Darron L West; and the stage manager was Martha Donaldson. The cast was as follows:

ELLEN .... Marin Ireland
DANNY .... Michael Chernus
KAYLA .... Susan Pourfar
LAURIE .... Danielle Skraastad
JUDY .... Deirdre O'Connell
AMY .... Jenny Bacon
TESSA .... Miriam F. Glover

IN THE WAKE was co-premiered at the Kirk Douglas Theatre/Center Theatre group in Los Angeles, California, opening on March 21, 2010 (under the title THE WAKE) and subsequently produced at Berkeley Repertory Theatre in Berkeley, California, opening on May 14, 2010. It was directed by Leigh Silverman; the set design was by David Korins; the costume design was by Meg Neville; the lighting and projection design were by Alexander V. Nichols; the sound design was by Cricket S. Meyers; and the stage manager was Elizabeth Atkinson. The cast was as follows:

ELLEN .... Heidi Schreck
DANNY .... Carson Elrod
KAYLA .... Andrea Frankle
LAURIE .... Danielle Skraastad
JUDY .... Deirdre O'Connell
AMY .... Emily Donahoe
TESSA .... Miriam F. Glover

DIALOGUE NOTATION

This is not a play of assertions. The thoughts and feelings of the characters should be evolving and fluid, taking shape in the back and forth of their conversations with each other. It should feel spontaneous. For Ellen in particular, it is imperative that her dialogue be driven by wonder, curiosity, and deep pleasure in her search for lucidity.

Double slashes (//) in the dialogue indicate the start of the next spoken line.

Ellipses are used here to indicate a character's active search for the right words or image.

PROJECTIONS

Projected images from television and print news are indicated in many of the transitions between scenes. These projections should be prominient, immersive and immediate. They are meant to pull the audience into a visceral memory of time and place, and to reconnect them with whatever assumptions and frame of mind they held at that time. The content of the projections should serve only this purpose. Though perhaps tempting, it is much better not to choose clips that score political points or invite the audience to easy judgment.

CHARACTERS

ELLEN, white, mid to late 30s, is funny, earnest and self-assured. She advocates for her ideas fiercely and with enjoyment, and she grapples eagerly with the ideas and the feelings of others. She is a delightful talker, charmingly self-aware, who often pokes fun at herself to soften her excesses—though she does not apologize for her passion. Her efforts to be big and good and responsible are sincere, as is her love for her family and friends.

DANNY, white, mid 30s, is Ellen's long-time boyfriend and Kayla's younger brother. He is a schoolteacher and exceptionally good at it, though low-key when talking about it. He is easy-going and understated—but not simple. He runs deep. He is confident about what matters to him and doesn't need his choices affirmed by others.

KAYLA, white, mid to late 30s, is Laurie's partner, Danny's older sister, and best friends with Ellen since they were in college, where she was Ellen's idol. She is a freelance writer of fiction and journalism. She supports herself with a series of day jobs at various not-for-profit social-justice organizations.

LAURIE, white, mid to late 30s, is Kayla's partner and works as a chef. She's fierce in her affections and loyalties and though she's sometimes irritable with Ellen she loves her as family. She finds talk of politics stressful, and the heated conversations that take place regularly in her home feel to her like a rigged competition she could never win if she cared to compete—which she doesn't. She is attractively dykey—altough she does *not* actually look like Ellen DeGeneres.

JUDY, white, mid 50s, is Ellen's long-time friend. She is an international aid worker and the kind of person who feels most at ease in a crisis zone. She has no romantic illusions that the world can be changed, but she also cannot pretend that everything is fine. It is important to note that there is no sense of betrayal in her critique of American democracy, since she never believed American democracy was intended to include people like her.

AMY, white, mid 30s to early 40s, is an experimental filmmaker who lives in Boston. She is intelligent and unselfconsciously direct in conversation. Feelings move through her unmediated, and she presents them without calculation.

TESSA, bi-racial, 16, is Judy's niece.

IN THE WAKE

ACT ONE

The present.

Lights up on Ellen. She's mid-thought in a conversation with her (unseen) friend, Judy, searching for a way to describe her confusion with the current state of things.

ELLEN. Have you ever known a moment like this? I haven't. I don't remember ever feeling like this. It's…an *incomprehensible time.* On the one hand everything seems fine. I mean, not fine, maybe, but recognizable. Like, not fine but you can see fine, you can see that fine is down the road. And on the other hand…it feels like nothing's fine; It's like we've crashed into a brick wall, full speed, and we're mortally wounded. We're sitting in this smashed up car and we're broken and bleeding—but, the thing that is so super weird about this moment is that somehow *we still think we're fine.* We're in the broken car and we're broken and we're, like, listening to the radio and, I don't know, sort of idly chatting about, hmm, what if this car crashes? And not registering that *it's already happened.* I mean… I don't know if that's happened. That's what I'm saying. Everything feels familiar and yet totally unrecognizable, and I don't know how to negotiate that. There must be a blind spot somewhere. You know what I mean? There's got to be some huge thing we're not seeing. Because if you can't figure out how you ended up so far off the path you thought you were on, it must be because there was some huge-ass thing you weren't seeing. Right? There must be a blind spot. I think that must be right. And I think we… Well… *I* have to look back over these past years and…suck it up…and try to find that blind spot.

Scene 1

PROJECTIONS: COVERAGE OF THE STILL UNDE-CIDED 2000 ELECTION

The projections iris down to the TV in Ellen and Danny's East Village apartment. It's Thanksgiving 2000.

Ellen stands, staring at the TV, transfixed, holding a phone in one hand and the remote in the other. Danny enters from the kitchen with paper Thanksgiving decorations and Scotch tape. He wraps his arms around Ellen from behind. He watches with her for a second.

DANNY. They're going to be here soon. *(Beat.)* You might want to think about turning that off.
ELLEN. I cannot believe the ruthlessness of the Republicans. Listen to this bullshit. It's… It's… It's… Oh my god, I can't believe it.
DANNY.   *(Singing a meandering, made-up song.) Happy Thanksgiving, it's a Happy Thanksgiving, where the turkeys run free, you should turn off the TV…*
ELLEN. *(Her focus on the TV unbroken.)* I will in a minute… *(The phone in Ellen's hand rings. She answers before the end of the first ring.)* Hey. *[…]* It means that even if the vote count changes to Gore's favor, the Florida State Legislature is going to send Republican delegates to the electoral college *[…]* Well, I assume if Gore has the votes his delegates would also go. *[…]* Yes, there'd be two opposing sets of delegates from Florida at the Electoral College, which, you know, *then* what happens? What? *[…]* Oh. *(To Danny.)* Turnips. Laurie // wants—
DANNY. They're ready.
ELLEN. *(Into the phone.)* The turnips are ready. *[…]* Yeah, I got celery. *[…]* What, is she doubting me? *[…]* No, okay. I'll double check. *(Handing Danny the phone, mock-offended.)* Laurie doesn't believe I got celery.
DANNY.   *(Teasing her.)* Well… *(Ellen gives him a look and goes to*

check.) Hello, my sister! How is Thanksgiving so far on the third floor? *[...]* Uh huh. *[...]* Oh! That sounds very nice. *[...]* Well. Here on the fifth floor, aka the CNN news desk—the presidential election is still hotly contested.

ELLEN. *(Taking the phone back.)* Give me that.

DANNY. "Special Coverage: A Nation Undecided" *(Impersonating dramatic "breaking news" music.) Chung-chung.*

ELLEN. *(Into the phone.)* You tell Laurie I got the celery, the lady apples, the cheese, and I got her mulling spices from her favorite guy at the farmer's market. *(The TV captures her attention again.)* Oh my god, Kayla, I'm going to lose my mind.

DANNY. Okay, soon we're going to have to switch into Thanksgiving mode.

ELLEN. Seriously? *(Into the phone.)* I know. What are we supposed to do? Pretend this isn't happening?

KAYLA. *(Entering carrying with a platter of food and talking into a phone tucked under her chin.)* I don't know. *(Danny takes the phone as she joins Ellen in front of the TV.)*

ELLEN. I mean, it's like nobody ever heard of a recount before this. It's like it's some diabolical invention that conniving, thieving Democrats have conjured from thin air.

KAYLA. I know. As if Democrats were cohesive or organized enough to carry out any sort of plan!

ELLEN. Oh my god, in our dreams.

DANNY. Ladies? Oh, ladies. *(He snaps his fingers to get their attention.)* Look at me. Look at me. *(They wrench their gazes away from the TV to look at him, a bit blankly.)* Focus... Focus... I'm advising you here to take a break from current events, just for today— *(Ellen starts to object.)* Whoa. Whoa. Easy. Easy there, James Carville. Laurie is going to be very unhappy if this thing takes over the whole day.

LAURIE. *(Calling from two flights down.) Kay?*

KAYLA. Oh. *(Yelling down to Laurie.)* Coming, honey. *(To Danny.)* You're right.

ELLEN. Okay, I know, you're right, it's just... *(Kayla and Ellen both get sucked back into the TV.)*

KAYLA. What is this, MSNBC?

ELLEN. Yeah. *(They watch.)*

KAYLA. What's on CNN? *(Ellen switches. They watch for a second.)* Aargh! No! I can't watch him.

ELLEN. Come back, Florida Supreme Court! Make them start counting again!

LAURIE. *(Calling from downstairs.) Kayla?*

DANNY. Do you want me to go?

KAYLA. Oh my god. No. *(Calling down.)* I'm coming!

ELLEN. You need help?

KAYLA. No, I got it. Be right back. *(She exits. Small beat.)*

DANNY. You didn't by any chance mention…

ELLEN. *(Understanding he means Judy.)* Not really.

DANNY. Hm.

ELLEN. What?

DANNY. Nothing.

ELLEN. What?

DANNY. You just might want to pick your battles today. You might want to think about keeping the political talk to a minimum.

ELLEN. Yes, I know. Laurie hates "political talk." Which basically means anything // on any subject—

DANNY. *(Making a dial-turning gesture.)* You know what I'm doing?

ELLEN. What?

DANNY. Dialing down…

the intensity.   ELLEN. …the intensity. Okay.

(Laurie and Kayla enter, with trays of food.)

KAYLA. We're back!

LAURIE. Happy Thanksgiving!

DANNY. Merry Thanksgiving!   ELLEN. Happy

Oh!— *(Danny remembers something.*   Thanksgiving!

Where is it?)

ELLEN. Laurie! It looks so good!

LAURIE. You know why? *(Laurie puts a bite of food into Ellen's mouth.)*

ELLEN. Oh my god it's so good!

LAURIE. It's really good. *(Danny gets his face dangerously close to the pie Laurie's holding.)* What are you doing?!

DANNY. I'm just going to lick it a little.

LAURIE. Off it! *(She takes the pie to the kitchen.)*

DANNY. *(Opening the box he's located.)* Look, we almost forgot!

ELLEN. Oh no.

DANNY. *(Taking from the box a pilgrim hat, putting it on.)* 'Tis family tradition.

KAYLA. 'Tis.

DANNY. *(Handing a pilgrim collar to Kayla.)* Prudence, for thee.

(And one to Ellen.) Mistress Quickly? Laurie, come out here. You don't have a pilgrim collar.

LAURIE. No, you know what I have instead?

DANNY. What?

LAURIE. Dignity. Okay, the turkey probably has…a half hour-ish… So… Ice.

DANNY. Okay, prepare yourself—I'm thinking we should put it in the tub.

LAURIE. Genius.

DANNY. Well, you don't learn shit like that at a SUNY school, do you?

LAURIE. Oh. You Oberlin motherfucker! You know what? That school is in *Ohio,* man. It's in *Ohio.* You know what I'm saying?

DANNY. Yes. That's why they call it "the Harvard of the Midwest." Race you downstairs.

LAURIE. *(Scoffs.)* Right. Like I'm gonna race. *(Suddenly makes a break for it.)* Sucker!

DANNY. Oh, I don't think so. *(He blasts out the door after her. We hear them chasing each other down the stairs, laughing. Kayla and Ellen look at each other.)*

ELLEN. Just for a minute. *(They turn the TV back on. They're immediately sucked in.)*

KAYLA. I don't think they're coming back.

ELLEN. They're just getting ice.

KAYLA. No, the Florida Supreme Court.

ELLEN. Oh right. Fuck. *(They remain glued to the TV as Laurie and Danny burst back in, laughing, with big bags of ice.)*

DANNY. I win!

LAURIE. I won! Oh my god, those stairs!

KAYLA. WHAT ARE YOU TALKING ABOUT, YOU ASSHOLE!?	ELLEN. IF IT WAS CLEAR HE'D WON THERE WOULDN'T BE A RECOUNT!

LAURIE. Oh no. *(To Danny.)* I cannot take a whole day of that.

ELLEN. *(Eyes not leaving the TV.)* We're turning it off, Laurie. We're going to turn it off right now.

KAYLA. We're turning it off now, honey. *(Reaches her hand out to Ellen for the remote.)* Here.

ELLEN. *(Reluctantly, eyes still on the TV.)* Okay. *(Kayla snatches the remote and clicks the TV off.)*

ELLEN. *(To Laurie.)* Your girlfriend is bossy.

LAURIE. Do you want to rephrase that?

ELLEN. Your girlfriend is really bossy. *(Laurie grabs Ellen's thumb and bends it back.)* Ow!

LAURIE. I cannot believe you. Say it.

ELLEN. Ow! What?

LAURIE. Say it!

ELLEN. Ow! Okay. Wife. Wife. Wife. Wife. Wife.

LAURIE. Don't do it again. *(She play-attacks Ellen.)*

ELLEN. Ow. Danny, protect me! *(Danny dives into the pile.)*

DANNY. Leave my woman alone, you she-devils!   LAURIE. Get off... Ow!   ELLEN. Ow! Ow!   KAYLA. Ow! My leg is crushed!

(Judy enters, looking like hell in slept-in clothes, and watches the screaming, laughing, wrestling group until, one by one, they realize she's there. A beat.)

JUDY. I was gonna take a shower. The tub's full of ice.

DANNY. Oh! Sorry, Judy. I'll take care of it. *(Danny exits to the bathroom. Judy follows him. Kayla and Laurie look at Ellen.)*

KAYLA. She's going someplace, right?

ELLEN. She is. She's going to her sister's in Kentucky.

KAYLA. But today.

ELLEN. I think she's gonna be with us today. *(Kayla and Laurie exchange a look.)* What? Is that alright?

KAYLA. What are we supposed to say, Ellen?

ELLEN. I know, I'm sorry, I'm sorry. I thought she was going right to Kentucky. But she got in really late last night.

KAYLA. And she assumed she was invited to spend Thanksgiving with us?

ELLEN. No, she didn't know it was Thanksgiving. She's been in Sierra Leone for, like, the past nine months and she had to come back so suddenly. I don't think she even knew what day it is.

KAYLA. But now that she knows, doesn't she want to be with her own family?

ELLEN. She doesn't get along with her family.

KAYLA. I don't get along with her.

ELLEN. Oh, Kayla.

KAYLA. I don't like her.

ELLEN. Kayla!

KAYLA. What? *(Off Ellen's look.)* Okay, I like her. It's the big "I grew up really poor and now I'm an aid worker in Africa so I know the world is really fucked up in ways you middle-class liberals can't imagine" stick she's got up her *ass* that I don't like. *(We hear the shower running. Danny reenters.)*

DANNY. I put the ice in the sink.

ELLEN. She came back to the States because her mother just died.

KAYLA. Oh. Great. Now I have to be nice to her.

DANNY. And…welcome to Thanksgiving, ladies and gentlemen!

ELLEN. Kayla.

KAYLA. I'm sorry. What I meant to say is, I really enjoy her warm company, she's totally interesting and she does really important work.

ELLEN. And that's true.

KAYLA. I know, Ellen. I temp at the same not-for-profit organizations you // do—

ELLEN. I know, I know—

KAYLA. *(Continuing.)* —I also know plenty of people who do human rights work but they don't look down on you if you're not up to date on every aspect of the political situation in whatever country they're working in.

ELLEN. Okay, I know she can be a little intense // sometimes.

LAURIE. A little?

ELLEN. I know. But I'm intense.

LAURIE. Not like her.   KAYLA. Not like she is.

ELLEN. Sure I am.

KAYLA. No, you're not. Judy's a… // a…

LAURIE. She's a total freaking buzz-kill.

KAYLA. Yes. And you… // are…

LAURIE. You just talk too much.

DANNY. *(Appreciative color commentary.)* Harsh toke.

LAURIE. What? She knows she talks too much.

ELLEN. *(Agreeing. It's a simple fact.)* I do.

LAURIE. The bottom line is she's not particularly relaxing to be around.

ELLEN. Well, Laurie, you're never relaxed with anyone outside your own demographic.

LAURIE. What?

ELLEN. Tell me who you socialize with who's not just like you?

LAURIE. You. Straight. // Eew.

ELLEN. Shut. Up.

KAYLA. The bottom line is you should have asked us.

13

ELLEN. I know. I know. I screwed up. I kept thinking something would—You know, that she'd have some plan for today. But she's not close to anybody else here, really. Her mother died. But you're right, you're right, you're right. You know what? *(Sincere.)* I'm going to ask her to go to a diner.

KAYLA. Ellen!

ELLEN. I'm sorry.

JUDY. *(Calling from the bathroom.)* Is there a towel?

KAYLA. *(To Ellen.)* Mad!

ELLEN. I'll get one for you. *(She exits.)*

DANNY. And the Pilgrims and the Indians sat down *together* in a feast of peace, and God rewarded the pilgrims with shiny // buckles on their shoes and to the Indians he gave maize—

ELLEN. *(Reentering.)* Hush. Hush. Hush. Hush. By the way, for the record, Laurie, I've been with girls.

LAURIE. *(Laughing.)* Oh, yeah.

ELLEN. What? I have.

KAYLA. One girl. In college. You made out.

ELLEN. Two! *(Kayla scoffs.)* Two! One of whom I dated for a month!

LAURIE. A whole month? News flash: You're married to a man!

ELLEN. I'm with Danny and we're not married.

DANNY. And Danny's…not a man…?

ELLEN. Honey, you are so manly! You make Arnold Schwarzenegger look like a little girl. *(Danny makes muscles and bares his teeth. Judy enters.)*

JUDY. What time is it?

ELLEN. Hey, honey.

DANNY. It's four-thirty.

ELLEN. Come in, sit down.

JUDY. Jesus Christ. I slept for…seventeen hours.

ELLEN. Long trip. You're totally jet-lagged.

JUDY. Wow, that's incredible. I never fucking sleep. Does anyone have a light?

ELLEN. Oh, honey. I'm so sorry. You can smoke on the fire escape if you want.

JUDY. *(A deep sigh of irritation.)* Okay. *(Muttering to herself on her way to the window.)* One good thing about a refugee camp, there may not be clean water but you can fucking smoke. *(She climbs out onto the fire escape and closes the window behind her. A beat.)*

KAYLA. You're right. I was wrong. She's really fun.

ELLEN. Oh, Kayla.

DANNY. Laurie! Turkey.

LAURIE. Oh! Right. *(A weary sigh, as she contemplates the stairs.)*

ELLEN. I'll go down and check it for you.

LAURIE. Oh yeah? Check it for what?

ELLEN. *(Sheepish.)* I can see if it's still there.

LAURIE. I hate living here.

ELLEN. Oh, you don't.

LAURIE. Five flights, Ellen.

ELLEN. You only live on three. Wait, that's not my strongest argument.

DANNY. Laurie. New plan.

LAURIE. *(Loves this game!)* New plan. Go.

DANNY. I'm thinking—Hear me out—You and I...are leaving the East Village and moving to... Ready...? The Bronx.

KAYLA. *(No way!)* The *Bronx!*   ELLEN. You gotta be kidding!

LAURIE. You're not coming. Just us. *(Back to Danny.)* Go on.

DANNY. An industrial ruin with good bones...

LAURIE. Love. Catering kitchen?

DANNY. *Bien sur!* And...on the roof...? Full suburban yard.

KAYLA. *(Sucked into the dream.)* For Slip 'N' Slide?

DANNY. Perhaps.

LAURIE. Oh, you want to come now?

KAYLA. If there's Slip 'N' Slide.

ELLEN. Hey, what about me?

LAURIE. You love it here.

DANNY. She might want to come, though—Because I could build for you—

ELLEN. What?

DANNY. Especially for you...

ELLEN. What?

DANNY. A soundproofed NPR listening room!!

ELLEN. Danny!

DANNY. That's how much I love you.

ELLEN. *(Putting her arms around Danny and kissing him.)* You are a kook. That sounds very, *(Kiss.)* very, *(Kiss.)* very *(Kiss.)* nice. *(Kiss. Judy returns and plops in a chair.)*

DANNY. My lady's totally into me, Judy. You see that?

JUDY. I see it. Is there any possibility of getting some coffee?

DANNY. There is, indeed. How do you take it?

JUDY. In an IV?

DANNY. Alright, then.

ELLEN. Oh wait, I bought good coffee. *(She follows Danny into the kitchen. Judy just stares, a little out of it. Kayla and Laurie wait, uncomfortably, for Judy to acknowledge them. A long beat.)*

KAYLA. Hey, Judy. *(A beat. No response.)* It's nice to see you again.

ELLEN. *(Coming from the kitchen to drop off spoons and napkins.)* Oh. You remember Kayla, Danny's sister? And her partner, wife, wife, wife, Laurie?

JUDY. Oh, yeah. Hi. How're you doing? *(Ellen returns to the kitchen.)*

KAYLA. We're glad you could join us today. How are you doing?

JUDY. Aside from feeling I've been run over by a tank? I'm peachy. *(Beat.)*

KAYLA. So you got back—when?

JUDY. Uh… Uh… Wednesday.

KAYLA. Yesterday.

JUDY. Yesterday… Yeah. So. Yeah.

KAYLA. We're very sorry to hear about your mother.

JUDY. *(A small bitter laugh.)* Oh. Yeah. I mean, thanks. *(A beat.)*

KAYLA. Ellen was saying you just got back from Sierra Leone. *(Ellen returns.)*

JUDY. Guinea.

ELLEN. Oh, I thought   KAYLA. Oh, I…
you said Sierra Leone.

JUDY. *(Matter of fact.)* The refugees are from Sierra Leone. Well, most of them. Some are Liberians, but most of them came up from Sierra Leone because they were being terrorized by the RUF—the Revolutionary United Front—obviously—and now they're being terrorized by the Guinean Security // Forces—

DANNY. *(Returning with Judy's coffee.)* Here you go.

JUDY. Thanks—So they're heading back to Sierra Leone where they'll be terrorized again by the RUF and then they'll come back to Guinea and…you know.

KAYLA. Yes. It's really…terrible. Or… I mean…

DANNY. *(A rhetorical question designed to charm and cajole Judy.)* Say, Judy, one of my students told me that Guinea is known as "the Switzerland of Africa." Is that true?

ELLEN. Danny—

JUDY. *(Bemused.)* Why yes, I believe there are those who refer to it as "the Switzerland of Africa." One of your students told you that? Is he Guinean?

DANNY. No, I believe he's Bed-Stuyvean.

ELLEN. It was Antwan, wasn't it?

KAYLA. Oh! Antwan!   LAURIE. Oh my god I love
                                                          that kid.

ELLEN. Tell Judy about Antwan. *(Prodding him. She loves this story.)* Tell her what he wore for his report.

DANNY. Well, Judy, young Antwan gave his report on Guinea wearing a cocktail dress he'd made himself out of Kente cloth.

JUDY. Wow.

DANNY. Yes. If he had any self-awareness at all he'd be the gay Rosa Parks of junior high.

ELLEN. Judy, you can't imagine how good Danny is with these kids.

DANNY. Yeah, yeah, yeah…

ELLEN. *(To Kayla.)* Why? Why does he scoff?

KAYLA. No, I know.

ELLEN. Why can he not accept what a great teacher he is?

DANNY. *(Mock-serious.)* I'm an astonishing teacher, Judy.

ELLEN. You are! Judy, you should see how the kids look at him. It's like he's… Like he's…King of the Teachers.

DANNY. *(Gazing into the middle distance.)* King…of the Teachers…

ELLEN. Okay—

DANNY. I like that.

ELLEN. Okay, never mind. Go back to what you were saying // about Guinea.

DANNY. I was saying…? I don't remember. I was crowned King of the Teachers…and it all // went black…

ELLEN. Judy, you must be hungry.

JUDY. Ich! No. I'd like some wine…

ELLEN. *(A bit taken aback.)* Oh, okay.

JUDY. I brought a bottle of wine for you. Didn't I hand it to you last night? *(Spying it across the room.)* Oh. There. *(Ellen retrieves it.)*

LAURIE. Can I see that? *(Taking the bottle.)* This is a great bottle of wine. *(Danny takes it to pour Judy a glass.)*

JUDY. *(Shrugs.)* Yes, French-speaking Africa has its amenities. Chad may be a shit-hole worse then Haiti but the croissants are divine.

LAURIE. Really?

JUDY. Better than Paris.

LAURIE. Hey, Danny, I'll have some of that.

KAYLA. Me too.   ELLEN. Yeah, me too.

JUDY. *(Inspecting the snacks on the coffee table. Pointing to one.)* I'll take some of that now. What is it?

ELLEN. It's Laurie's famous artichoke dip.

JUDY. *(Suddenly recoiling.)* Oh. Never mind. *(Small beat.)* Oh, by the way, I keep forgetting to ask, who's the new president? *(Beat. No one knows how to respond. Is she joking?)*

DANNY. Well, I'm King of the Teachers. *(A beat.)*

JUDY. No, but who is it?

ELLEN. Are you serious?

JUDY. Yeah.

KAYLA. Do you not get news there?

JUDY. American news? Not much.

ELLEN. The election isn't settled.

JUDY. Whaddya mean?

ELLEN. Do you really not know this? Florida's contested and they're trying to figure out how to recount. It's a mess.

DANNY. I'm pissed at Gore.

ELLEN. Gore??   KAYLA. Oh, Danny!

DANNY. Yeah. All he had to do was appear to be a reasonable facsimile of a human and instead he was like some freaky, obsequious robot.

LAURIE. Obsequious Robot! I love that band! *(Danny sings a riff of a made-up song as the made-up band Obsequious Robot.)*

ELLEN. It's actually really bad, Judy.

LAURIE. *(Weary of this argument before it's even happened.)* It's a mess, but it's always a fucking mess.

KAYLA. Yeah, but a lot is on the line this time. Bush sucks.

LAURIE. He does suck, but I think they both suck.

ELLEN. They're really, really not equivalent, Laurie.

LAURIE. *(To Judy.)* They're pissed off at me because I voted for Nader.

KAYLA. That's not true. You can vote for whoever you want to vote for.   ELLEN. I'm fine about it. New York's not a swing state.   DANNY. I voted for Angelina Jolie.

LAURIE. Who'd you vote for, Judy?

KAYLA. Laurie!

LAURIE. What? I'm curious.

JUDY. I didn't vote.

ELLEN. Not absentee?

KAYLA. She was in Sierra Leone, Guinea, Guinea.

LAURIE. Listen, between the two of them I hope Gore wins but people were freaked out about Nixon, they were freaked out about Reagan, and in the end it didn't really make that much of a difference.

JUDY. *(An aside to whomever.)* I think the Chileans and the Nicaraguans might argue with you on that point.

ELLEN. Exactly.

LAURIE. Alright, whatever. I'm just telling you my opinion. They're *both* in the pocket of the corporations, they're both equally unfriendly to gay people—

ELLEN. The Democrats may not be stellar on gay issues but // they're certainly better than—

LAURIE. Bill Clinton crawled up the asses of gay voters // before the election, and the first thing he did in office was Don't Ask/Don't Tell.

DANNY. Gay voters love that. Seriously.

ELLEN. Yes, that sucked. But you do know the Religious Right // wants much worse than that.

LAURIE. All I'm saying is that Democrats and Republicans play exactly the same games. For instance—let's be real about this whole manual recount thing.

ELLEN. *(Wary.)* What?

LAURIE. Come on, Ellen, if you're honest about it, you have to admit that the Republicans have a valid point.

ELLEN. About what?

LAURIE. Ellen, how is running the cards through the machines not more fair and neutral than a manual recount?

ELLEN. I... I can't... I don't even know how...

LAURIE. What's more non-partisan than a machine?

ELLEN. Kayla, Kayla, Kayla, please help me explain to your girlfriend // that the Republican—

LAURIE. Why? Why's she gotta cut me like that?

ELLEN. Wife, wife, wife. Okay, sorry, sorry, wife. Laurie, the Republican rhetoric around the hand recounts is *outrageous.* MANUAL RECOUNTS ARE STANDARD. ACCEPTED. THEY'RE WHAT YOU DO WHEN AN ELECTION IS CONTESTED. GEORGE BUSH HIMSELF SIGNED MANUAL RECOUNTS INTO LAW IN TEXAS. OF COURSE HE DID. NINE OUT OF TEN TIMES THE VOTER'S INTENT ON THOSE CARDS // IS TOTALLY CLEAR.

LAURIE. *(To Danny.)* Oh man, what did I do?

ELLEN. But I'm going to tell you something—

LAURIE. Oh, fantastic.

ELLEN. The big thing being exposed here is not about Bush or Gore in Florida. What I really think // is that—

LAURIE. Hey, we're finally going to hear what she really thinks.

ELLEN. Yes, you are, Laurie. You started it // What I really think is that while we're—

DANNY. *(To Laurie.)* All on you.

ELLEN. *(Continuing on.)* —While we're paying obsessive attention to minutiae like the Republican operatives who said they saw Democratic poll workers eating chads—

KAYLA. I know, that is crazy.

ELLEN. Yes, but the point is, we're missing the big story, which is that nationwide tens of thousands of voters are being *systematically disenfranchised.* As a *rule* in poor and minority areas, thousands of people cast ballots that are *never counted.* What has been laid bare in this past few weeks is that we don't know who's actually been elected *ANYWHERE.* And we don't seem to care. And you're right, Laurie—

LAURIE. I am?

ELLEN. —Oh, now you pay attention—This is as true on the left as on the right. We like the *idea* of democracy. We love it. But only in the *abstract.* None of us is interested in anything as boring and unsexy as the realistic *maintenance* of it. George Bush becoming president would be scary, but do you know what's really scary?

LAURIE. *(To Danny.)* Yeah, that electro-shock thing in Cheney's chest.

DANNY. *(To Laurie.)* No. No. Anne Heche showing up at your house acting all crazy.

ELLEN. Ah ha ha. *(Sulking.)* Never mind. *(Laurie sees, oops, they went too far.)*

LAURIE. We're sorry.

ELLEN. *(Pouting.)* No, forget it.

DANNY. *(Taking Ellen's head in his hands like it's a cute stuffed animal.)* Look at this brain! Even now, in one of the very rare moments where she's not actually talking, this brain is going 120 miles per hour. Exhausting. And *irresistible.* I would like to take a bite out of this head. I *love* it. I need to bite it. *(He play-bites her head.)*

ELLEN. *(Waving him off.)* Okay, stop that. What's really scary is the Republicans are questioning the *legitimacy of the system.*

LAURIE. Okay, this one's on // you!

DANNY. You're totally right. // How much do I owe you?

ELLEN. Listen, you! Listen up! James Baker is *dismissing the Florida Supreme Court as an illegitimate body* because they ordered a statewide recount and *he doesn't like it.* And that's *TOTALLY* frightening. Do you understand this? Because I am telling you—the only thing that makes us different from Bosnia or Rwanda or Nazi // Germany is that we—

KAYLA. Whoa, whoa, whoa! Many things make us different from Rwanda and Nazi Germany, // Ellen.

ELLEN. What makes us different is that we all agree to operate within the rules of the system. But once we jump that rail we are in serious trouble.

KAYLA. Come on, Ellen, those countries have totally different histories than we // do—

ELLEN. Yes // but—

KAYLA. Germany was in a state of total instability following World War I; // Rwanda…has ethnic divisions that // predate their colonial period.

ELLEN. Okay, yes, but…Kayla, do you remember watching the Winter Olympics in Sarajevo? Do you think they saw what was coming?

KAYLA. Ellen, again, again, that came out of a completely different set of circumstances // than anything that's happening here—

ELLEN. What I'm saying, what I'm saying is that the circumstances here, right now are very precarious. And unless you feel Americans have some inherent, *biological* advantage—

KAYLA. Oh, come on, Ellen, you know that I // don't think that—

ELLEN. —or that by virtue of being American we're inherently good, then I don't know why you would assume things can't spiral out of control.

KAYLA. Ellen, American democracy is a deeply culturally embedded system. It's not a new system, it's not a superficially // imposed system—

ELLEN. That doesn't mean nothing bad can ever happen // to us—

KAYLA. Ellen, that's not what I'm saying.

ELLEN. Kayla, the rhetoric of the past few days is *terrifying* to me.

KAYLA. Yes, it's infuriating, it's partisan, it's *wrong,* but your analysis is—It's a little unhinged. // Yes. I think you need to take a step back.

ELLEN. No. No. No. Kayla, I think this is something we haven't seen before.

KAYLA. Maybe it is…but… We are never going to be Rwanda.

ELLEN. Kayla. There is a ruthless dismantling of the system happening here. Seriously, seriously, listen to me. *They Don't Want to Recount the Votes.* They don't even *pretend* to respect the *Established Channels of Democracy.* And I'm telling you, if we decide there are no rules—Look at that map of the red states and the blue states—I'm *telling* you—Go ahead and scoff, Laurie, but I'm telling you it's the queer people who are going to get pushed into the ocean first. *(Beat.)*

KAYLA. Pushed into the ocean??

ELLEN. Okay. Stop laughing at me. I know I'm ranting, I know I'm driving everybody crazy.

KAYLA. Oh, you're not.

ELLEN. I know I am, shut up you. I know you love me. The best thing about me is that I understand what's so irritating about me. I know sound like a crazy Cassandra. Although I do think it's pure delusion to assume this country will right itself no matter what, okay, okay, laugh away. I hope you're still laughing in two years, that's all I have to say. *(Half a beat.)* Where's Judy?

KAYLA. Maybe she's making us a festive holiday centerpiece.

DANNY. She's probably smoking.

ELLEN. I better go check on her.

LAURIE. *(Jumping up.)* Oh my god! I never checked the turkey! Shit.

KAYLA. Want me to go with you?

LAURIE. Yeah. We can probably start to think about eating. Danny, come too. We'll bring everything up. *(Laurie, Kayla and Danny exit. Ellen finds Judy on the fire escape, smoking. She grabs a sweater and climbs out to join her.)*

ELLEN. Hey, here you are.

JUDY. Here I am.

ELLEN. You okay?

JUDY. Yeah.

ELLEN. Ooh. It's nice to get some air. Let me have a drag off that. *(Judy hands her the cigarette.)*

ELLEN. A lot of family energy in there, huh?

JUDY. *(A beat.)* Gimme that. *(Ellen hands the cigarette back. Judy takes a drag.)*

ELLEN. Shouldn't be too long until dinner. Laurie's checking the turkey— *(Judy's cell phone rings.)*

JUDY. *(Searching frantically.)* Where is it? Where is it? Christ, why is it so small? Where the fuck is it? *(She finds it, opens it and sees the caller.)* Oh fuck. *(It keeps ringing.)*

ELLEN. Should I go so you can answer it?

JUDY. No. It's my sister.

ELLEN. Do you want to turn it off?

JUDY. Uh… Well—I'm waiting for a call.

ELLEN. Oh. Well, stop the ringer. *(She reaches for the phone.)* Here.

JUDY. Don't answer it.

ELLEN. *(She pushes a button and the ringing stops. She hands the phone back.)* Here.

JUDY. Huh. I just got it, I don't know how it…

ELLEN. I know, you with a cell phone. It's like Benjamin Franklin with a video game.

JUDY. Yeah, like that.

ELLEN. It's good your sister can reach you.

JUDY. Good, hell. I can't wait to give this thing back to the colleague I borrowed it from. Then he can deal with her. Ha. I don't know why I gave her the number. I know better. She's called me four times already. Yesterday she called me from the funeral home in Corbin, telling me I had to send her money because if I didn't Mom was going to be buried in the "welfare coffin."

ELLEN. What's that?

JUDY. There's no such thing. That's what the funeral director called it to shame her into buying a more expensive one.

ELLEN. That's horrible!

JUDY. *(Shrugging it off.)* Fucker.

ELLEN. What did you do?

JUDY. I told her no.

ELLEN. Oh. *(A beat.)* So how're you feeling about going home?

JUDY. Like it's going to suck. *(A beat.)*

ELLEN. Judy, do you want me to go to this funeral with you?

JUDY. What? No.

ELLEN. Maybe I should.

JUDY. That's crazy.

ELLEN. Why is it crazy? It's one of the perks of my freewheeling itinerant lifestyle. Four different jobs. I can ditch any of them.

JUDY. Where are you working these days?

ELLEN. Subject changer.

JUDY. You still at Amnesty?

ELLEN. Every once in a while.

JUDY. They miss me?

ELLEN. Oh, terribly.

JUDY. How's your writing?

ELLEN. Judy…

JUDY. How's your writing?

ELLEN. *(Letting her off the hook, for now.)* My writing's…fine. I'm starting to think finally about writing about my infrastructure obsession.

JUDY. Your…

ELLEN. You know, my thing that everyone finds so dull they can't hear my voice when I'm talking about it: the tax code, the regulatory structure…

JUDY. Oh, yes, of course.

ELLEN. Kayla's been telling me since we were sophomores in college that I should write about it. I should probably just do what she tells me. You know she just had a story published in *Ploughshares?*

JUDY. *(Surprised. Didn't think Kayla had it in her.)* Huh.

DANNY. *(Popping his head through the window.)* Ladies—

ELLEN. *(Starting to get up.)* Time?

DANNY. No, no. Kayla's gone to the Indian grocery.

ELLEN. She has?

DANNY. Apparently she was supposed to get cardamom yesterday— so there's a bit of tension…

ELLEN. Oh no.

DANNY. I'm guessing when she gets back there might be a little "processing."

ELLEN. Oh God…

DANNY. So I just wanted to let you know you have a few more minutes to enjoy the patio.

ELLEN. Okay, keep us posted. *(Danny goes back in. A small beat.)* Did you get that whole "wife" thing between those two earlier? You know they had a big wedding.

JUDY. No, I didn't know that.

ELLEN. Oh yes. June. Full-on. You should have seen it. Every member of Danny and Kayla's big Irish Catholic family was there, weeping, drinking…

JUDY. Sorry I missed it.

ELLEN. I mean it was lovely but… *(A reflective beat.)* Nobody from Laurie's family showed up except for her mother.

JUDY. Oh dear.

ELLEN. Her father wouldn't come. It broke her heart, it was terrible. Danny's family, on the other hand, was looking at me the whole time, like—The lesbians are getting married, for Christ's sake! What's wrong with you?! *(Judy laughs. A reflective beat.)* I just don't get the whole wedding thing. I never got it. I didn't fantasize about it when I was a kid. Did you?

JUDY. I mostly fantasized about having my own house. And a gun. And a horse.

ELLEN. Nice. *(Beat.)* What's the automatic reverence for marriage?

JUDY. You're asking the wrong person. It didn't do a thing for me.

ELLEN. I think I'm just not a romantic person. I don't know. This is what I fantasized about when I was a kid—what I have now—this big family jumble, this puppy pile of people. I was such a solitary kid.

JUDY. I had a whole gang.

ELLEN. You did?

JUDY. Yeah. I ran 'em.

ELLEN. I bet you did. *(Beat.)* Judy, I'm really sorry about your mother.

JUDY. Oh…yeah…

ELLEN. When was the last time you talked to her?

JUDY. Eight years ago.

ELLEN. Long time.

JUDY. Yep. *(Beat. Ellen gives her space to talk.)* Yeah, it was after I got back from Timor. Yeah. And…I just couldn't… I got there and Eileen was in the hospital—

ELLEN. Your sister.

JUDY. Yep—because her husband Gene had really done a job on her…and I thought that I'd talked her into leaving him…and my mother talked her into staying. And I was done. My niece Tessa was…*six,* she was six, God, she'd be fourteen now. Yeah…and I was not interested in watching her go through what we did and they were never going to change, so…

ELLEN. It's too bad you can't pick your parents.

JUDY. Gene's not Tessa's father.

ELLEN. Oh.

JUDY. No. No, Tessa's father is black. Apparently. *(Judy's phone rings again. She jumps. She digs it out of her pocket.)* Shit! Come on, come on, come on. *(She peers at the phone. She hits the button.)* Hello? Larry? Hello? *(She looks at the phone again.)* Hello? *(The call is gone.)* Shit. *(She stares at the phone for a moment.)* He has to call me back, I can't call him. So fucking frustrating!

ELLEN. Who's Larry?

JUDY. *(Neutral.)* A friend.

ELLEN. A friend.

JUDY. He's my housemate.

ELLEN. Your housemate?

JUDY. Am I not speaking English?

ELLEN. You're not living in the camp.

JUDY. I'm living in town.

ELLEN. In town?

JUDY. Are you just going to repeat every thing I say?

ELLEN. It's just that you usually... I mean, I thought... I think it's good.

JUDY. You think what's good?

ELLEN. I don't know, Judy! What are we talking about? God! You're frustrating!

JUDY. I'm living with Larry.

ELLEN. Like...*(Judy doesn't fill in.)* Like... Is he your boyfriend?

JUDY. Boyfriend? I'm fifty-six years old! Boyfriend.

ELLEN. Okay, is he...

JUDY. We're lovers. *(Beat.)*

ELLEN. Well, that's... That's really nice, Judy.

JUDY. How do you know? You don't know him.

ELLEN. *(Bemused, but really asking.)* You're right. You tell me. Is it nice?

JUDY. Yeah it's nice. It's no big deal.

ELLEN. How did you meet him?

JUDY. He's an economic development guy. He's Australian. He's based at the London School of Economics but he has a research fellowship at the University of Conakry.

ELLEN. How long have you been seeing each other?

JUDY. About five months.

ELLEN. It's... It's nice that while you're here dealing with all of this, he's there waiting for you.

JUDY. Yeah. *(Beat.)* He's actually leaving for London tomorrow. He's spending December there with his family.

ELLEN. *(Carefully judgment-free.)* Oh. He's married?

JUDY. Yes. Things happen in conflict zones. It's a different thing there.

ELLEN. No, no, I know. I always just want more for you.

JUDY. For me this is more. *(Judy's phone rings again.)*

ELLEN. Larry?

JUDY. *(Looking at the phone.)* It's my fucking sister. *(She hands it to Ellen, who turns off the ringer.)*

ELLEN. I'm going to the funeral with you.

JUDY. You can't go with me.

ELLEN. You can't go there by yourself. Listen, it should be a law. After a certain point no one should ever go home without a reality-check companion. You have to let me come.

JUDY. Maybe I should.

ELLEN. Yes. Judy. It's done. I'm coming with you.

JUDY. Alright.

ELLEN. Good. *(Small beat.)* I should probably check in. You comin'?

JUDY. In a minute. *(Ellen climbs back into the kitchen. Then sticks her head back out.)*

ELLEN. Hey. I'm glad you're here.

JUDY. Oh yeah, I'm fun at a party. *(Ellen goes into the front room where Danny is on the couch, watching football.)*

ELLEN. They're not back?

DANNY. Not yet. Wanna make out?

ELLEN. You think they're okay?

DANNY. They're fine. *(He gestures for her to come sit next to him. She curls up against him.)* How's your pal?

ELLEN. She's okay. *(Beat.)* I made Kayla and Laurie mad.

DANNY. You might have irritated them a little.

ELLEN. You tried to tell me.

DANNY. I tried.

ELLEN. When am I going to listen to you?

DANNY. That's what I want to know.

ELLEN. I do listen to you.

DANNY. Sometimes. Sometimes you do.

ELLEN. I told Judy I'd go with her to her mother's funeral.

DANNY. You did? How come?

ELLEN. Her family's terrible. She's so alone. Do you think it was a good idea to tell her I'd go?

DANNY. I think if your friend needs you, you should go.

ELLEN. Do you want to come along?

DANNY. Nope.

ELLEN. Didn't think so. *(Small beat.)* She's got a new boyfriend.

DANNY. Go Judy.

ELLEN. A married guy.

DANNY. Ah.

ELLEN. What do you think?

DANNY. I don't know anything about it. But I do know that people gotta do what people gotta do. *(They sit together, watching the TV.)*

ELLEN. What is this?

DANNY. Football. Ever heard of it?

ELLEN. I know it's football. Who's winning?

DANNY. The Vikings.

ELLEN. Vikings. Good team. They have a really deep bench. Who're they playing?

DANNY. The Cowboys.

ELLEN. Cowboys. Good team. They have a really deep bench.

DANNY. That joke is so lame. *(Beat.)*

ELLEN. Danny? We're so lucky.

DANNY. Shit yeah.

Scene 2

PROJECTIONS: COVERAGE OF THE SUPREME COURT DECISION IN BUSH V. GORE AND AL GORE'S CONCESSION, URGING THE NATION TO SUPPORT THE NEW PRESIDENT.

It is May 2001, six months later.

Ellen and Amy sit in a lounge area outside a lecture hall somewhere on the Harvard campus. They are deep in conversation.

AMY. *(Trying to figure out...)* But... But... Wait. I'm lost. I thought you said you were writing about strip malls.

ELLEN. No, no, I'm writing about the *tax code*—

AMY. Okay?

ELLEN. —My *example* is strip malls.

AMY. *(Amy thinks about this, then—)* More.

ELLEN. Okay.

AMY. Okay.

ELLEN. Stick with me—

AMY. I will.

ELLEN. —'cause this is good.

AMY. I believe you.

ELLEN. Alright, the thing people don't realize about strip malls is that the reason they're everywhere is that in the 1950s Congress made a *tiny* change to the tax code, accelerating the depreciation rate for new construction—

AMY. Okay...?

ELLEN. And the reason they put it there was to encourage manufacturing, but what it *actually* did was create a tax *loophole* that made it profitable for developers to build strip malls in non-populated areas. And *that's* why strip malls are everywhere. These boring little infrastructures *matter.*

AMY. Aha.

ELLEN. But we don't see it. Because Americans are dedicated to the myth that we're all operating independently, and I'm not just talking about motherfucking libertarians who think all humans act in a self-interested vacuum, Alan Greenspan and his Ayn Rand bullshit—fucking libertarians drive me crazy—No, no, no, I'm talking about *us* on the *left.* Somehow we are *incapable* of thinking systemically or politically. Our whole strategy seems to be to find some magic personality to make it 1968 again, while—Okay, okay, okay, this is the thing: Somebody *is* thinking systemically and it's Karl Rove, and the Club for Growth guys. While *we're* putting all of our energy into praying for another Kennedy, *they* are making a million tiny changes to the tax code, to media regulation, to anti-trust protections, to election laws, and they are successfully channelling money, power and votes their way and we can't figure out what is going on. We're like "Waaaait a minute. Waaait a minute. What's going on?" These systems *matter* because... because... because, look—when the American Revolution was over, the logical thing for the framers to do would have been to say: "Okay. King George is out, our guy is in, thank you very much, now go back to your...candle-dipping." But they had this *vision* of a dynamic society and they believed the only way to create that was *systemically.* All those brilliant men and they didn't just put one of them in charge. Instead they created this *system,* this carefully constructed series of *conduits* through which people's energies and aspirations could *flow.*

It's the thing that just…*moves* me about this country. It's the thing that just…just *slays* me about this country—that it was set up to be a place where people could *change*—that the whole idea was to allow people to change their status, change their lives—Was that your question? I'm sorry, I got off track, what was your question again?

AMY. You have a beautiful mouth.

ELLEN. What?

AMY. You have a beautiful mouth. People must tell you that.

ELLEN. What? Uh. No. Not so much.

AMY. I really like watching you talk.

ELLEN. *(Flustered.)* Good thing. I talk a lot.

AMY. I'm sorry. Go on.

ELLEN. Well, I lost my train of thought.

AMY. The framers?

ELLEN. The framers…the framers…I don't know. I can't remember what I was saying. *(Looks around, startled.)* Weren't there a lot of people here? Where did everybody go?

AMY. I don't know.

ELLEN. My ass hurts!

AMY. I think we've been sitting here a while.

ELLEN. What time is it? Didn't the panel just end? It's dark out.

AMY. *(Looks at her watch.)* It's nine. We've been here four hours.

ELLEN. Really? Oh my god. Wow. I talk a lot! I'm sure you wanna get home. Or to your studio. Do you work late? You probably want to get back to your clay.

AMY. Clay?

ELLEN. I don't know why I assumed clay. What kind of sculpture do you do?

AMY. *(Amused.)* I'm a filmmaker.

ELLEN. How did I get sculptor?

AMY. I have no idea.

ELLEN. Sculptor. Hmm. Do you sculpt *anything?*

AMY. No.

ELLEN. Did you tell me you were a filmmaker?

AMY. Yeah.

ELLEN. I'm sorry.

AMY. It's okay. I called you out of the blue when I saw you were coming to Harvard.

ELLEN. I'm so embarrassed. Okay, so films. About what? Did you tell me that already, too?

AMY. No. Uh…
films I'm known fo...
are collections of fl...
short—a minute each. ...
ELLEN. What are they ...
AMY. They're… Ah. If I c...
so many more grants. I actu...
them too much. I want them ...
ELLEN. Huh. *(A beat.)*
AMY. Were you surprised when I...
ELLEN. I don't know. Yeah.
AMY. You remembered me.
ELLEN. Well…yeah, I mean. When... ...m
college your sister gave us daily reports. ... ... in the
debate team. She was so dazzled by you.
AMY. Yeah, well…
ELLEN. I'm surprised you remember me.
AMY. I remember you because you seemed so…brave.
ELLEN. Brave? Me? I was afraid of everything all the time.
AMY. Really?
ELLEN. I had to teach myself to be brave.
AMY. How do you do that?
ELLEN. I don't know…At some point I thought—if I get to the
end of my life and realize I didn't do all these things because I was
afraid I'm going to be so pissed. I couldn't bear that. *(A beat.)*
AMY. You think a lot.
ELLEN. I do.
AMY. I feel a lot. Too much, really.
ELLEN. How can you feel too much? I can't imagine it. *(Amy shrugs.)*
AMY. My sister showed me that article about you in the *Times*.
ELLEN. Wow. She must read the *Times* really carefully.
AMY. Well, she was very impressed.
ELLEN. How's she doing?
AMY. She's good. She's married. Three kids. My dad lives down
the street from them—He moved there when my mom passed
away a few of years ago. They're all family, family…And… I think
I'm not really cut out for that kind of family life.
ELLEN. Not everybody wants the same kind of life.
AMY. Yeah. No, I want it. I want it a lot, actually. But maybe not,
you know. Maybe not really, or I'd have it, right?

...ybe you just don't have it yet.

...right.

...n't have to talk about it.

...talk about it.

...ply.) I don't want to. (A small beat.)

...N. So…you said you're doing something new with your films?

AMY. I did?

ELLEN. I thought // you did—

AMY. Oh yeah. Yeah. Uh… Well…I've been thinking about negative space…or, I mean, my relationship to negative space.

ELLEN. Negative space…?

AMY. It's… Have you ever taken a drawing class?

ELLEN. No.

AMY. Me neither, actually. But I was teaching myself to draw—

ELLEN. You were? That's so industrious.

AMY. Is it?

ELLEN. I'm sorry. Go on.

AMY. —Well, there's a basic exercise you do when you're learning to draw where you draw the negative space.

ELLEN. Which means…?

AMY. It means you don't focus on the object you're drawing, you draw the space around it. So if I was drawing your hand— (Taking Ellen's hand in hers.) I wouldn't draw your fingers. Instead I'd look at the shapes of these spaces between your fingers— (Tracing those shapes.) This is negative space. Your hand is positive space. And when you draw with this exercise, the drawings are…almost unsettling, they're so vivid You really see the thing. You really see the hand. Somehow by focusing on what it's not, you end up with an intense…an intense sense of what it is.

ELLEN. (Flustered, taking her hand back.) Oh. Uh-huh.

AMY. Negative space is also an idea in architecture. It's open space. Space that's…undefined. It makes people uncomfortable. They instinctively move toward positive spaces where the boundaries are clear. It's not unrelated to what you were saying before about Jane Jacobs.

ELLEN. Oh, Jane Jacobs. I do love her so.

AMY. Well, of course you do. She's all about infrastructure and flow. I always want to make the Intelligent Design people read her.

ELLEN. Why?

AMY. Because… Okay, their central argument is: There must have been a plan. And Jane Jacobs says the opposite. She says that cities only work when they're not completely planned, when there's space for unplanned juxtapositions and unexpected encounters…for randomness.

ELLEN. Yes.

AMY. *(Building this idea.)* And…it's… It's such an important idea. Because any artist will tell you, any scientist will tell you, that it's the accident, it's the mistake, that causes you to re-frame and expand everything. Nothing really amazing is created by one mind thinking rationally. The "intelligent design" argument is absurd! How could something so complex and amazing as the universe come from one rational mind? But nothing really extraordinary happens without some irrational leap. We don't leave our comfort zone easily right? People who want to lead big lives and think big thoughts—they know, a wrench in the works, well, it might not be pleasant but it will get them to the next place. They're willing to let themselves be knocked off track.

ELLEN. I agree, but for some reason people are afraid of that.

AMY. Some of them. Yes. Well, of course they are.

ELLEN. Why?

AMY. Because…flux is very uncomfortable.

ELLEN. But I don't get it. You can think you're choosing certainty but you get strip malls and George Bush. How can that be more comfortable?

AMY. Lots of people grapple with complexity. But…complexity is scary.

ELLEN. To me it feels obvious.

AMY. The things that matter, the huge, magnificent things, the big three. Art, Religion…Sex… Each of them can take us to the highest place. Or the lowest. You know? Each of them offers transcendence. And also degradation. I think probably that's what makes them…the biggest things.

ELLEN. You're very smart. You're a smarty-pants. *(Amy shrugs. A little embarrassed. A beat.)*

AMY. Are you and Danny planning to have kids?

ELLEN. No. Kayla and Laurie are.

AMY. But not you?

ELLEN. Maybe. I don't know. I feel…I'm ambivalent. It's that thing of wanting to stay open to the injection of randomness.

AMY. I think having kids is probably one injection of randomness after another, actually.

ELLEN. Probably so. Yes, that makes sense. We talk about it sometimes. Maybe we will. Are you thinking you want to have kids?

AMY. I want so much. *(A beat.)* Wanna hear something funny?

ELLEN. What.

AMY. When I saw that piece about you in the *Times,* I thought: That's the person I'm going to marry. And then, one second later, I thought: Oh. No. She's already married.

ELLEN. That is funny.

AMY. I know. And so I called you.

ELLEN. Well. Huh.

AMY. Yeah. It's funny. *(A beat.)*

ELLEN. I'm not speechless that often.

AMY. It's okay. I know you're with Danny. I just wanted to see you. I'm glad that I called you.

ELLEN. I'm glad, too. I didn't really know you then—it's funny—as kids. But I feel now—I don't know—something…familiar…?

AMY. Yes. *(A beat.)* I feel kind of scared.

ELLEN. You do? Why?

AMY. I don't know. It's okay. *(Ellen shakes her in a jokey way.)*

ELLEN. You! What's going on here?

AMY. I don't know. Something. *(Ellen lets go of her.)*

AMY. How many more days are you in Boston?

ELLEN. Four.

AMY. Huh.

ELLEN. What? *(Amy gives her a look.)*

ELLEN. I know. I have to get the hell out of town! *(Amy takes Ellen's face in her hands. She captures Ellen's gaze and holds it. She leans in to kiss her. It's a moment of electric intensity. Amy breaks the kiss. They're both a little stunned.)*

AMY. I shouldn't have done that.

ELLEN. No. It's okay.

AMY. I'm a little slain by you.

ELLEN. I'm… I'm…

AMY. I feel a little overwhelmed. I feel a little scared.

ELLEN. Oh no. It's okay. This—um. You know. Nothing is happening. I mean—This is…this is probably the best part anyway. Right? I mean…this part is probably better than sex.

AMY. *(Direct, sincere.)* Oh no, I'm sure sex would be much better.

Scene 3

A few months later. Five A.M.

Ellen has just woken in her hotel room. She picks up the phone and dials. Amy, sleeping, in Boston, picks up.

AMY. Hello?

ELLEN. Hey. It's me.

AMY. Hey. Hey, you. *(A sleepy beat.)* What's going on?

ELLEN. Nothing. I…

AMY. What time is it?

ELLEN. It's late. It's the middle of the night.

AMY. Oh… I was dreaming.

ELLEN. You were?

AMY. Yeah… *(Progressively remembering.)* My family was on a picnic…on a…boat? And… It's kind of hard to describe—My mother was…kind of there but kind of not? And then…somehow… *(Amazed.)* you were there.

ELLEN. I was?

AMY. *(Remembering.)* You found me.

ELLEN. I did?

AMY. I was…I didn't know where I was. And you came and got me.

ELLEN. I did?

AMY. And you put your arms around me. And you held me. You held me. *(Wondrous feeling.)* Even right now, I feel like you're holding me.

ELLEN. *(Feels it physically. Amazed.)* I know. I feel it too.

AMY. You do?

ELLEN. Yes. You woke me up. Do you know that? I was sleeping and I felt you shake me awake.

AMY. I did?

ELLEN. I feel like you did.

AMY. *(Drifting back into sleep, so happy.)* Oh. That's so nice.

Scene 4

PROJECTIONS: COVERAGE OF BUSH'S SPEECH FROM THE RUBBLE PILE, ALERTS ON AIRLINE SECURITY, GULIANI URGING PEOPLE TO GO ON WITH THEIR DAILY LIVES.

January 29, 2002.

On the fire escape, Judy smokes, jumpy. Ellen, in the kitchen, wearing her coat, pours two glasses of wine.

JUDY. *(Calling in to her.)* What time is it again?
ELLEN. Five minutes since the last time you // asked.
JUDY. Okay, okay.
ELLEN. *(Climbing out to join her.)* They're going to be here any second.
JUDY. We cannot miss that nine o'clock train.
ELLEN. I know, Judy. But it's six.
JUDY. We should have just taken the earlier train. Tessa has to get up so goddamn early for school—We didn't need Larry to pick us up—we could have taken a cab.
ELLEN. You will make your train. I promise you.
JUDY. Okay. *(Ellen hands her the wine.)* Thanks.
ELLEN. How is the dashing Larry?
JUDY. ...Fine.
ELLEN. Uh-oh. What's happening?
JUDY. Nothing.... Exactly what I knew was going to happen. I knew it was a bad idea from the minute he got that World Bank job and started in about me finding a job in D.C. I knew it was a bad idea. What'd someone say to me one time...? Don't sign up for pain? I signed right up.
ELLEN. Well, you didn't know that Tessa was going to come live with you.
JUDY. I did not.
ELLEN. So...It's a whole different situation.

JUDY. Why did I take her?

ELLEN. Because she asked. Is she a problem for Larry?

JUDY. Are you kidding? Larry's fine with Tessa. She's just a problem for me.

ELLEN. You are helping her. *(Off Judy's look.)* You are. She's with you and not her bat-shit mother. You got her into an excellent school. You know this tutor Danny set her up with today is considered The Guy for kids struggling with math.

JUDY. I think you don't know how different this world is from hers.

ELLEN. But that's the point, isn't it? She wants a different life.

JUDY. Maybe.

ELLEN. Judy, this is a girl who had the wherewithal to track you down in—wherever the hell you were—

JUDY. Senegal.

ELLEN. Yes, and ask to come live with you.

JUDY. She's out of her league.

ELLEN. Judy, she's doing fine.

JUDY. *(Looking at her watch.)* Didn't they pick her up from the tutor at two-thirty?

ELLEN. *(Reminding her.)* Then they went to the Tenement Museum—

JUDY. It's six o'clock.

ELLEN. Danny got excited. He's showing her the city. *(Reassuring her.)* Kayla and Laurie promised they'd get her back in plenty of time. That's why I sent them.

JUDY. I don't know how you live so close to people. *(Ellen laughs.)* How do you handle your situation with Amy with them living right on top of you?

ELLEN. *(Realizing this.)* I think... I think we've developed some sort of unspoken agreement not to talk about it.

JUDY. They know?

ELLEN. *(She would have thought this was obvious.)* Yeah. Oh yeah, it's not a sneaking around kind of a thing.

JUDY. Oh.

ELLEN. But, we don't really talk about it. *(Realizing this herself as she's saying it.)* They can't make sense of how Danny and I could possibly be working this out between us, so... So, yeah, they know but...I think they prefer to steer clear of the subject.

JUDY. Seems like a lot of work.

ELLEN.   *(Laughs.)* I suppose. *(Thinks for a beat. Then:)* Something happened to me that night I met Amy. Sitting with her—just talking—I could feel myself...*open.* I don't know how else to describe it—I literally felt something unlock and open. Like a whole part of me I didn't even know existed—it woke up. And I realized that a part of me had been dead. How could that be, you know? *(Thinks for a beat.)* ...Because what I have with Danny is more than most people ever dream of. We have...*daily joy.* That's extraordinary. There is daily happiness in my life with Danny. Who gets that, you know? There's nobody I love being with more than him.

JUDY. So... What's your plan?

ELLEN.   *(Wryly amused.)* My plan. Hmm. *(Thinks for a small beat.)* I think about choosing...and it's like...I could cut off my arm or I could cut off my leg. I don't have a plan, per se, but... I do know that this configuration isn't sustainable. I can't be in two places at one time. That's not okay. But something will change. These relationships are so different. I don't know what's going to happen. Something we can't see yet. Yeah... *(Sound of the group coming in the door.)* Hey, they're back!

JUDY. Oh, thank god.

LAURIE. Hey! Hello!   KAYLA. Hello! We're back! Where is everybody!

DANNY. Tessa has conquered New York!

TESSA.   *(To Kayla re: Laurie.)* I want her to say it again.

LAURIE. What, my professional opinion?

TESSA. Yeah. *(Laurie makes a dramatic vomiting sound.)*

KAYLA. *(Laughing.)* Laurie stop that! Tessa, I apologize for Laurie!

TESSA. She's okay.

DANNY. Uh, Tessa, she is definitely not okay.

LAURIE. Thank you, Tessa!

ELLEN. Hey everybody.

TESSA. Hey.

ELLEN. How was your afternoon, Tessa?

TESSA. Pretty fun.

DANNY. Not according to Laurie.

ELLEN. Where have you guys been? *(Laurie pretends to vomit.)*

TESSA.   *(Trying to remember the name.)* Uh...

KAYLA. We went to Congee Village.

ELLEN. Congee Village???

DANNY. Tessa loved it. It's her new favorite restaurant.

LAURIE. Did you love it, Tessa?

TESSA. Not really.

DANNY. Ah! Like a dagger in my heart!

LAURIE. Where do you take someone when you're showing them New York—Empire State Building? *(Danny fake falls asleep, snores.)* Statue of Liberty? *(More snoring.)* Or to eat disgusting porridge at Congee Village.

DANNY. *(Popping awake.)* Congee Village?

LAURIE. Danny, congee is a viscous, watery rice porridge.

DANNY. Laurie, millions of Chinese people love congee.

LAURIE. Yes, Danny, and millions of Americans love Hot Pockets.

DANNY. Hot Pockets. Mmmmm.

LAURIE. Tessa, tell Ellen about the Tenement Museum.

ELLEN. Was it fun?

TESSA. It was fine.

LAURIE. Tell her what you said.

TESSA. About...?

LAURIE. You said the Tenement Museum reminded you of something.

TESSA. Oh yeah. This apartment. *(Kayla, Laurie and Danny laugh.)*

ELLEN. Oh, ha ha ha.

TESSA. Why is that funny?

LAURIE. Because Ellen doesn't want to admit that she lives in a craphouse.

TESSA. I didn't mean it like that.

ELLEN. We know.   LAURIE. I'm teasing her.

JUDY. *(Entering.)* Hey, Tessa.

TESSA. Hey, Aunt Judy.

LAURIE. *(Prompting her.)* Hey, Tessa...do you want to give...

TESSA. Oh!! *(She digs through her backpack, pulls out a shopping bag, and hands it to Judy.)* Here. *(Judy, takes it. Tessa waits.)* It's from the Tenement Museum. It's a present.

JUDY. Oh. Thank you.

TESSA. You're not going to open it?

JUDY. Oh, did you want me to open it?

TESSA. I don't care. *(Judy opens it and pulls out a large men's Tenement Museum T-shirt.)*

JUDY. That's very nice. Thank you.

ELLEN. That's a great shirt.

JUDY. It is. Thank you, Tessa.

TESSA. *(To Kayla and Laurie.)* I told you she wouldn't like it.

JUDY. I like it. Quite a bit.

KAYLA. *(To Laurie.)* Where are we with dinner?

LAURIE. Ooh, yeah. Tessa? Ready?

TESSA. Oh. Oh, yeah.

LAURIE. Have your stuff?

TESSA. *(Retrieves her grocery bag.)* Yep.

LAURIE. Okay, we'll be back in a few minutes. Plates. Silverware. Be ready when we get back.

ELLEN. On it. *(Laurie and Tessa exit.)*

LAURIE. *(Offstage.)* Argh! Look at this crapped out hall, Tessa. It looks exactly like the Tenement Museum!

ELLEN. *(As soon as the door is closed and Tessa is out of range, to Danny.)* So, how'd it go?

DANNY. The tutor said Tessa did great.

JUDY. Oh. Uh-huh?

ELLEN. What'd he say?

DANNY. He said he tested her and her basic math skills are for shit, which we knew already. But he said her aptitude is normal and with help he doesn't see any reason she shouldn't be at grade level by the end of the year.

ELLEN. That's great.

KAYLA. Isn't it?

JUDY. Yeah. That's good news.

KAYLA. She's a great kid, Judy.

JUDY. Is she?

KAYLA. Yeah. She's…Yeah.

JUDY. Yeah. She's…she's a good girl. *(Beat.)* I'm gonna go smoke.

ELLEN. Okay. I'll come get you when dinner's here.

KAYLA. It's cold out there. Do you want a scarf or something? *(Judy exits, closing the fire escape window behind her.)*

KAYLA. Wow. She's a regular Carol Brady.

ELLEN. Okay… But you know Tessa's much better off with Judy than she was in Corbin.

KAYLA. I guess.

ELLEN. *(Remembering her task)* Okay. Okay. What do we need here?

KAYLA. Oh, right!

ELLEN. Plates.

DANNY. Beer? *(They start to gather the dinner things.)*

to one of the programs at ~~Youth Horizons.~~

ELLEN. Speaking of which—we need an update on our favorite anal-retentive boss, aka Tidy McSphincterstein.

KAYLA. He quit!

ELLEN. He quit??? When???

KAYLA. Like, two weeks ago.

ELLEN. Tidy McSphincterstein quit two weeks ago and you didn't tell me.

KAYLA. You weren't here.

ELLEN. Oh, right. *Who* is going to replace Tidy McSphincterstein?

KAYLA. His name is Tony McSwiggin!

ELLEN. That's what I said.

KAYLA. They actually want me to become the database manager.

ELLEN. *(Scoffing.)* Oh yeah, I bet they do.

KAYLA. I've been kind of thinking about it.

ELLEN. Okay… Why?

KAYLA. 'Cause…I'm already doing it. Part time. If I took the job I'd get a salary, have health insurance, two weeks paid vacation…

ELLEN. So…you'd have a steady paycheck, but… I mean, obviously that would be great, but what you need is time to write and freedom to prioritize that.

KAYLA. Yeah, you're right. I know, I know. I was just, you know…I was just thinking about it.

ELLEN. No, I know, it's tempting. *(Phone rings.)* Oh, yay, dinner!

DANNY. *(Racing for the phone.)* No! I got it! I got it! Me! No, me! It's mine. *(He picks up.)* Bongiorno. *[…]* Excellent! We'll be right down. *(He hangs up.)* Ready. *(Kayla starts to get up.)*

ELLEN. Kayla, you sit. We'll go. *(Ellen and Danny exit. Much to Kayla's horror, Judy comes inside and sits. A beat.)*

KAYLA. So… It's nice to see you Judy. *(No discernable response from Judy.)* So you're in D.C., now.

JUDY. Yep.

KAYLA. That's quite a change. *(Beat.)* How's your…? I'm sorry, I should know this, What's your job there?

JUDY. Consulting work with USAID.

KAYLA. Oh, oh, right. Right. USAID. Yeah. How is it working there?

JUDY. Well, I succumbed to a one-year contract even though I dislike D.C. intensely and shudder at the thought that Colin Powell's my boss…

41

KAYLA. Sounds challenging.

JUDY. Really? Compared to what I'm used to, I was thinking of it as kind of a break.

KAYLA. Yes, that's what I…um…meant…or…uh… *(Laurie, Ellen, Danny and Tessa enter with food.)*

KAYLA. *(Flooded with relief.)* Oh, good! Great! Good! Yum! This all looks so good! *(Re: a platter.)* Tessa, is this what you made for us?

TESSA. Yep.

KAYLA. It looks delicious! *(All agree. Throughout the serving of the food, the dialogue should be full and overlapping and responsive dialogue can be added to create this fullness.)*

DANNY. *(Taking the platter from Tessa.)* I'll take that. Thank you very much Tessa. What are the rest of you eating?

LAURIE. Let's eat it while it's hot.

TESSA. *(To Kayla.)* Can I sit by you?

KAYLA. Of course you can!

DANNY. Beer?

LAURIE. I'm having wine.

DANNY. Tessa, you want your Coke?

TESSA. Yes, thank you.

LAURIE. Hand me that plate, please, thank you. A little of everything?

JUDY. Thank you.

LAURIE. Not a problem. Tessa, do you want any salad?

TESSA. No. Thank you.

LAURIE. You don't want to just try a little.

TESSA. Maybe a little. *(Laurie puts some on her plate.)* That's enough.

LAURIE. *(Laughing.)* Okay.

ELLEN. This is a beautiful meal! Thanks you guys.

LAURIE. You're welcome. So this is a dish Tessa invented. And she wanted to make it for us tonight, and she just whipped it up down there like magic.

TESSA. It seems like it would take a long time but it's so fast.

KAYLA. How do you make it.

TESSA. It's Poppin' Fresh biscuits and then you cut a hot dog into pieces—

LAURIE. We substituted turkey dogs this time.

TESSA. Yeah, they taste alright.

LAURIE. Yeah, they're pretty good.

TESSA. And then you sprinkle grated cheese on top and that's it!

(Everyone "mmm"s supportively.)

TESSA. I make this for Aunt Judy like, four times a week. *(Everyone quickly arranges their face into an impressed response.)*

KAYLA. Mmmm. It's really, really good.

TESSA. *(To Laurie re: her dish.)* This is good, too.

LAURIE. It's Thai food.

TESSA. Oh! I like Thai food.

LAURIE. I *love* Thai food.

TESSA. There's a place right down the block from Aunt Judy's apartment we order from. I could eat from there every night.

LAURIE. You really like Thai food.

TESSA. I do. You can't get it in Corbin.

KAYLA. Do you love D.C.? Have you been to the National Portrait Gallery yet? It's my favorite.

TESSA. Uh-uh.

KAYLA. Ooh, what about the Smithsonian?

LAURIE. Whatever with the museums! Tessa, are you a Harry Potter fan?

TESSA. I love Harry Potter!

LAURIE. Aha! I knew it! Harry Potter rules!

DANNY. Rules! *(Re: Ellen and Kayla.)* These two ladies have never read Harry Potter.

TESSA. You *haven't?* *(They shake their heads.)* Why not???

DANNY. Snobs.   LAURIE. Snooty, stuck-up snobs.

ELLEN. I tried! I tried! I couldn't get past the third page!

TESSA. Why not?

DANNY. Snooty, snooty   LAURIE. Could not be more
super snobs.   stuck-up, snootier snobs if they tried.

TESSA. *(Suddenly scrutinizes Laurie.)* Who do you look like???

LAURIE. Me?

TESSA. All day long I keep thinking you look like somebody. Who *is* it? *(To the others.)* Doesn't she look like somebody famous?

DANNY. Burt Reynolds?

TESSA. No! *(Studies Laurie.)* Who do you look like? Oh! Oh! I know. I know who it is!

KAYLA. Who?

TESSA. It's that girl from that show. You know, that comedy show that's on TV. What's her name...? What's her name? Oh! Oh! I know. Ellen! *(Beat.)*

LAURIE. *(Bemused. Not sure how to respond.)* Huh. *(Beat.)*

43

DANNY. Come to think of it, you *do* look like Ellen. I don't know *what* it is…

LAURIE. Shut up. Shut up.

TESSA. Aunt Judy, don't you think she looks like her?

JUDY. I have no idea who that is.

TESSA. It's not a bad thing. I like her.

LAURIE. Yeah… No, we like her, too.

TESSA. I mean, I don't like her lifestyle, but…*(Beat.)*

LAURIE. Huh.

TESSA. What?

LAURIE. Um… Nothing… It's just that…

KAYLA. Tessa, uh… Laurie and I…are a couple.

TESSA. Oh. *(Getting it.)* Oh.

LAURIE. We're married, actually.

DANNY. Can you believe it?

TESSA. Y'all are teasing me. *(To Judy.)* Are they teasing me?

JUDY. *(At a loss.)* Well…they're gay.

TESSA. Oh…Well, that's cool.

KAYLA. We assumed that you…we assumed you knew that.

TESSA. Oh no. I didn't.

LAURIE. That'd be a small apartment for two people who aren't married.

TESSA. Oh yeah. Yeah. I…didn't think of that. I never met any gay people before.

JUDY. Come on, there are gay people in Corbin.

TESSA. Who?

JUDY. *(Suddenly on the spot.)* Well…I don't know, I can't think of any names, I haven't lived there in 40 years, there are gay people there, Tessa.

TESSA. Not that I ever met, Aunt Judy.

KAYLA. You know what, Tessa? There probably are gay people in Corbin but most likely they're in the closet. Which is a term // that's used to describe—

TESSA. I know. I know what it is.

KAYLA. Yeah. Okay. So… Well, particularly in small towns it can be difficult if you—I mean, you probably know much more about this than I do, it can be difficult if you don't fit in.

LAURIE. Yeah, you must have felt that way in Corbin.

TESSA. I'm not gay.

LAURIE. Oh, no.   KAYLA. No, no, that's not what she meant.

44

TESSA. I'm sorry, I don't understand. Can we talk about something else?

ELLEN. *(Warm, unsentimental, simple.)* We're fine, honey, I think they were saying that because you're black and Corbin is mostly white, you probably know what it feels like to be different.

KAYLA. Okay, okay, Ellen.

ELLEN. It's okay, Kayla. It's not a secret.

TESSA. But...I'm mixed.

ELLEN. I'm sorry, honey, what?

TESSA. I'm not different. My mother is white. I'm mixed.

ELLEN. Right, right, right. Yes. That's true.

DANNY. Hey, what happened to that drawing // you were going to show me? What's up with that? You holding out on me?

KAYLA. Hey, that's right.   LAURIE. Oh yeah.

TESSA. Oh. Oh yeah. My Celtic // knots.

DANNY. Aye, the knots!

TESSA. Aunt Judy, where's my backpack?

JUDY. *(Looking around.)* Oh...   KAYLA. Oh. It's over there.

TESSA. *(Retrieving the backpack and fishing out a folder with an elaborate Celtic knot design drawn on the back.)* Oh, thanks.

DANNY. So this was for what class again?

TESSA. Creative Arts. *(She displays her drawing. All ooh and aah and compliment her.)* They were hard to learn, but now I can't stop drawing them.

ELLEN. Can I see? *(Tessa hands the folder to Ellen.)*

KAYLA. What other classes are you taking?

TESSA. Um... Latin...

DANNY. Es-yay. Atin-Lay. Oh, you mean beginning Latin. Not the advanced Pig Latin.

KAYLA. Quiet, you. Okay, Art, Latin, what else?

ELLEN. *(Reading the title on the other side of the folder.)* "Government and Politics."

TESSA. *(With chagrin.)* Oh yeah.

ELLEN. *(Re: the contents of the folder.)* Can I look?

TESSA. Sure.

KAYLA. You don't like that class?

TESSA. No, it's...

KAYLA. What?

TESSA. Nothing. *(They wait for her to say more.)* I don't have the right opinions.

45

ELLEN. *(Apalled.)* Who says that??

TESSA. *(Shrugging.)* The other kids.

KAYLA. Well… What do you do in the class?

TESSA. We…read newspapers and, like, *Time* magazine and…

ELLEN. *(Re: a photocopied page from the folder.)* The president's State of the Union.

TESSA. Yeah.

KAYLA. *(Taking it from Ellen and looking it over.)* Oh yeah.

ELLEN. Remember that?

KAYLA. Oh yeah.

ELLEN. —In which he informed us that no other country likes freedom or dignity. We're the only ones. God chose us. We're just automatically good, no matter what we do.

TESSA. Yeah.

KAYLA. Okay, so you read these things and then do you…write papers? Have discussions? Or…? *(Tessa shrugs.)*

DANNY. You know what, Tessa?

TESSA. What?

DANNY. Those other kids are full of shit.

KAYLA. Danny…

DANNY. *(Stage whispering to Tessa.)* Oops. I'm not supposed to say the shit word.

TESSA. It's just that I don't know the right ways to talk about politics, and other kids do.

DANNY. I can guarantee you those other kids don't know as much as you think they do.

TESSA. Really?

DANNY. Guarantee.

ELLEN. Tessa. I get told all the time to keep my opinions to myself—

TESSA. You do?

ELLEN. Yes. And I ignore it. Just ask Laurie. There is no right way to talk about politics!

TESSA. I just… I just can't understand why everyone is so against him.

ELLEN. Against who?

TESSA. President Bush. *(Beat.)*

ELLEN. *(Doing her very best to be non-judgmental.)* Oh.

TESSA. I mean…in Corbin, on 9/11, we were all so scared. The thing that got me the most was that the teachers were crying, which, I was just like… I was just like Oh my God! I was just…praying and

46

praying and praying… And I remember the teachers explained to us, because we were like, why is this happening? Why are the terrorists attacking us? And they told us: No reason except they hate us. Just like you said, Ellen, they hate us because of our freedoms. So, when I got to D.C. I was like, Oh my God. *This* is where terrorists blew up the Pentagon. People died here on 9/11. I can't imagine how it felt to be there that day. But I do know if I had been there I would be like, Thank you, President Bush! Thank you for protecting us! And last week I said that in class. And people…just went crazy. Saying about how I'm stupid and I don't know anything about politics, so… *(Shrugging.)* It's okay. I don't have to talk in class anymore.

ELLEN. That is…inexcusable. *(A long, quiet beat. Then:)* But I think maybe you misunderstood me a little bit, Tessa. I'm actually not sure George Bush is protecting us. What I was meaning to say, actually, is that he kind of manipulated people after 9/11 to make them feel scared and angry.

KAYLA. Ellen…

ELLEN. What?

KAYLA. *(Attemptibg to lightly shift the conversation.)* Just…

ELLEN. What??

TESSA. Now people are upset.

ELLEN. We're not upset, Tessa.   KAYLA. You haven't made
                                  anyone upset, Tessa.

KAYLA. *(Still light.)* Ellen's just, always has to make her point.

ELLEN. I'm responding to her, Kayla. We're having a conversation.

TESSA. No, see, I shouldn't have talked about that.

ELLEN. Tessa, we're interested   KAYLA. We're fine, Tessa. You
in what you think.   did not upset us.

TESSA. Y'all think I'm stupid.

DANNY. Nope.	ELLEN. We	KAYLA. Tessa,	LAURIE. Oh
That's wrong.	absolutely do	you are amazing,	my god, Tessa.
	not! I am very	and we adore	*(Fierce.)* We do
	interested in	you.	not think
	what you were		you're stupid.
	saying.		And…I think
			that…actually
			you described
			something that
			I feel a lot.

TESSA. I did?

47

LAURIE. Yeah... *(Keeping it light and about Tessa, though she doesn't often talk about this.)* I work down near Ground Zero // and—
TESSA. You do?
LAURIE. Yeah. Yeah, the restaurant where I work is down there, // and—
TESSA. *(Wide-eyed, awed.)* Were you there on 9/11?
LAURIE. I was. Yeah. And...I've felt scared and angry...a lot...since then. And... Yeah, I don't feel like it's George Bush making me feel that way. So, yeah. I really... I can really appreciate what you said.
ELLEN. Oh, Laurie, that's not what I meant. I wasn't talking about regular fear.
LAURIE. What's regular fear?
ELLEN. It's... You know what I mean. Laurie, come on, you *(Judy's cell phone rings.)* know what I mean.
JUDY. Shit! Where's my phone? *(Everyone starts to look for the phone.)*
KAYLA. Is it...? ELLEN. I don't know.
JUDY. *(Finds it.)* Hello? [...] We're taking the 9 o'clock. // Tessa, get your stuff ready.
ELLEN. Is it Larry?
TESSA. But she was // telling—
JUDY. Tessa, please. *(Tessa goes to get her stuff. Back to Larry.)* Yes, I'm here. No, yes, // we can make it.
ELLEN. What's happening?
JUDY. *(Hangs up.)* Okay, where's my satchel?
ELLEN. You're leaving?
JUDY. Now Larry needs to meet the earlier train.
ELLEN. Is everything // okay?
JUDY. Satchel.
ELLEN. I think it's in the bedroom. *(Judy exits. To Laurie.)* What's going on? *(Laurie shrugs—nothing.)* I just wanted to respond to what she said and not patronize her. *(Tessa returns, studying a framed photo.)*
KAYLA. Hey, what have you got there?
TESSA. *(Caught.)* Oh...
KAYLA. That's our wedding picture.
TESSA. It is? *(Kayla nods. Tessa again studies the picture.)* Y'all got married in a church.
KAYLA. We did. *(Tessa examines the photo. Then, finally.)*
TESSA. I like your dress.

48

KAYLA. Thanks.

JUDY. *(Reentering, to Tessa.)* Ready?

TESSA. Wait. *(To Ellen and Danny.)* Where's y'all's wedding picture?

JUDY. Tessa—

TESSA. One minute. *(To Ellen and Danny.)* I wanna see y'all's wedding picture.

ELLEN. We're not married, Tessa.

TESSA. *(She looks at Ellen and Danny, then at Kayla and Laurie.)* Y'all are married and they're not?

LAURIE. Yep.

TESSA. How come they're not married?

LAURIE. *(Beat.)* You have to ask them.

TESSA. Don't you want to marry her, Danny?

DANNY. Depends how big her dowry is.

TESSA. Ellen, don't you love Danny?

ELLEN. I do.

TESSA. *(Thoroughly confused.)* Then why aren't you two married?

ELLEN. *(Searching for an appropriate, instructive response.)* It's… It's a big…question…

JUDY. Not everybody wants to get married, Tessa. Sometimes there are other ways people choose to be together.

TESSA. Oh… Like you and Larry?

DANNY. *(Falling over.)* Whoa, Tessa! You're killing us here!

TESSA. What???

KAYLA. Oh, honey!

JUDY. It's time to go. // We have to go.

ELLEN. Yes. Run. *(Hugging Judy.)* You're going to be fine. *(Kayla and Laurie help Tessa with her coat and backpack.)*

KAYLA. We're going to see you again really soon.

LAURIE. You have to come back and see *Harry Potter* with me.

TESSA. Okay. If I can.

LAURIE. What do you mean, if you can! You better come back, you stinker.

KAYLA. Okay, you gotta go. Scoot.

ALL. Bye. Bye. Safe home.

ELLEN. You've got plenty of time, Judy. You're going to be fine.

DANNY. Judy, we'll talk about another tutoring session, okay?

JUDY. Oh. Yeah. Thank you, Danny.

DANNY. Not a problem. You will be getting my bill. And it will be exorbitant.

KAYLA. *(Seeing the T-shirt bag, handing it to Judy.)* Oh. Judy, don't forget this.

JUDY. What? Oh. Yeah. *(Judy and Tessa exit.)*

ELLEN. *(Closing the door after them. Turning back to the group.)* Okay then. *(Everyone starts to clear the dishes.)* No, leave 'em. Leave 'em. I'll do 'em later. Coffee and dessert?

LAURIE. Oh. I'm tired. I think I'm probably going to go down.

ELLEN. Oh. Really?

LAURIE. Yeah.

KAYLA. Yeah. I'm tired too.

ELLEN. Oh.

KAYLA. Yeah.

LAURIE. You can stay if you want.

KAYLA. No, no, I'll come down with you.

ELLEN. Oh. Okay. Well… Hey, when are we seeing each other again?

KAYLA. Aren't we having dinner tomorrow?

ELLEN. Oh. Oh. Shit! I… I can't.

KAYLA. Oh.

ELLEN. I'm on that panel at the New School.

KAYLA. Oh right. Right. I should come to that.

ELLEN. Oh you don't have to. I mean, I'd love to have you there, but you've heard it all before.

KAYLA. I might like to hear the other people.

ELLEN. Oh, of course. Duh. Yes. Come. You should come. *(Beat.)* Listen, I'm sorry tonight wasn't…you know… That it was…you know. Laurie—

LAURIE. What?

ELLEN. I don't know. *(Laurie gives a shrug which says she's fine. Nothing to talk about. She turns to leave.)* I'm sorry.

LAURIE. For what?

ELLEN. I don't know, but you're mad at me.

LAURIE. I'm not. I'm fine.

ELLEN. Okay.

LAURIE. I'm not mad.

ELLEN. Okay.

LAURIE. I'm just… You know. *(She shrugs, turns to go, then:)* By the way…what is, um… What is regular fear?

ELLEN. *(Not immediately registering the reference.)* What? Oh. I don't know. Nothing. It was a bad word choice.

50

LAURIE. *(Working against her rage to stay cool and light.)* Yeah. 'Cause…"regular"—Nothing felt regular if you were down there that day.

ELLEN. No, of course not.

LAURIE. And…just so you know, I actually do feel afraid and angry, a lot of the time…so…

ELLEN. Of course. Laurie. Of course. I totally understand. I mean, come on, I'm angry all the time.

LAURIE. *(Doing her best to shrug it off and keep it light.)* Okay. Never mind.

ELLEN. *(Sincerely wanting to know.)* Laurie, what? Tell me. *(No response.)* Laurie, I really do understand.

LAURIE. Well, you don't, actually, because you weren't here; you were off with your girlfriend // you know—Okay, doesn't matter. You weren't here.

| DANNY. Whoa, whoa… | KAYLA. Laurie! | ELLEN. I wasn't— I was in Denver at a conference. |

LAURIE. Okay, okay, it's not a big deal, I was just pointing out that it's—It was different if you were here. It was different for people who were down there. That's… That's all I was saying.

ELLEN. I do know that, Laurie. I do know that's true.

LAURIE. Yeah. I mean… And, anyway, you know, I'm just not sure you're the ethical standard // bearer.

| DANNY. Whoa, how 'bout you take it down a notch. | KAYLA. Laurie! |

LAURIE. What, okay, I know we're all supposed to be fine with…all of it…and that's how it is and it pisses me off and okay, okay, okay. I get it. I'm fine. // I'm fine. I'm fine.

KAYLA. Laurie // *Laurie…!*

ELLEN. No, no, no. It's okay. It's a complicated situation…that I'm in. And she gets to have her feelings about it. Laurie, I'm sorry I used that term, it *was* dismissive, and it was…stupid. And, *truly*, Laurie, I'm sorry. *(Laurie grabs Ellen's shoulders and slow-motion shakes her – then accepts Ellen's hug, and fiercely hugs her back.)*

DANNY. A dinner plan?

| ELLEN. Oh, right. | KAYLA. Right. Right. |

KAYLA. Can you do Thursday?

ELLEN. Totally.

KAYLA. *(To Laurie.)* Honey?

LAURIE. Yeah.

DANNY. Thursday, Thursday—Ooh. I'm going to have to have my people call your people on that.

DANNY. I'm just not sure. I think I'm back from Switzerland by then and I know Michelle Pfeiffer wanted to have lunch with me but she always wants to have lunch with me so I think I can probably get out of it.

KAYLA. Oh my god, he's unbearable.

ELLEN. He's absolutely incapable of not making a joke. It wouldn't matter what the circumstance was.

KAYLA. Been like that his whole life, I'm here to tell you.

LAURIE. Danny! Shut up! Shut up!

KAYLA. Okay. We're going see you Thursday.

DANNY. Oh! Laurie! I have a request. You know what I want you to make for us Thursday?

LAURIE. What?

DANNY. Congee.

LAURIE. You know what? I'm going to make you fucking congee.

DANNY. That'll be so great. Because I. Love. Congee.

LAURIE. Night you guys. *(All say goodnight. Kayla and Laurie exit.)*

ELLEN. Night you guys. *(Danny closes the door after them. A beat.)*

DANNY. Just… Don't worry about it.

ELLEN. Am I an asshole? Am I just a total asshole? *(Danny makes a gesture meaning "let it go.")*

ELLEN. What was that, I don't understand being angry? Come on, I'm angry all the time!

DANNY. Well…

ELLEN. What?

DANNY. There's a difference between intellectual anger and wanting to kill somebody. *(Ellen thinks about this and takes in the fact that he's right—and, in this one way, she probably was an asshole.)*

ELLEN. Okay. Okay, yes. I can see that. I can see that. But you know what? Okay, it was a stupid word choice. Granted. Granted. But there is a difference between the trauma that Laurie feels, and I know she feels it, it kills me, it kills me how shaken she still is— But there is a difference between that and the manipulative fear-mongering Bush and company are promoting!

DANNY. I know.

ELLEN. I know you know, I'm sorry, I don't know why I'm yelling

52

at you. Because they're so judgmental, that's why, and it pisses me off!

DANNY. I know.

ELLEN. I know, you just let it slide off your back and // I should…

DANNY. It pisses me off.

ELLEN. It does?

DANNY. Yeah. Of course. They've decided I'm a victim. But… There's nothing I can do about it.

ELLEN. We can…be really angry.

DANNY. *(Laughing.)* Yeah, okay.

ELLEN. I don't like the way they judge us.

DANNY. Oh well. They don't want our life. But we don't want theirs either.

ELLEN. They've decided you're the victim and I'm the…bad one. They have no idea you had an affair. What would happen to their neat little analysis if they knew that? Their brains would explode.

DANNY. I presume you're talking about Claire?

ELLEN. Yes.

DANNY. It didn't really get that far, you know.

ELLEN. I know, but—

DANNY. I mean… She was *totally* into me.

ELLEN. I know.

DANNY. By the way.

ELLEN. I know she was. *(Small beat.)* It was a real thing that happened, though.

DANNY. Yeah. Yeah, I mean, for a while I did think it might be good for me to be with someone more regular // and I could have—

ELLEN. Regular?

DANNY. Uh…yes, Ellen, regular—And it seemed like I could have had that with Claire. *(Beat.)* But…then she wasn't you. *(Ellen throws her arms around him.)* I don't know *why* you're the one that I want but it seems like there's nothin' I can do about it. *(They sit. Her arms wrapped around him. A beat.)*

ELLEN. *(Sitting up to look at him.)* How are we doing, Danny?

DANNY. *(Getting up, suddenly cranky.)* Okay, enough! Do not let them // bother you!

ELLEN. No, this isn't about them. It's not. It's about us. I'm checking in.

DANNY. About what?

ELLEN. About us. You need to tell me…how you are. You know that, right?

DANNY. I do.

ELLEN. Okay. *(He holds out his hand to shake hers—deal. She keeps hold of his hand, holding his gaze steady.)*

DANNY. I don't like it. You know that, right? *(She nods slightly.)* But if I told you to stop—You have to play this out. I get that. You have to go through it...so you know...you want to be with me. *(Ellen nods.)* Hey. You're freakin' lucky.

ELLEN. I know. *(Beat.)* Thank you Danny, for being // so—

DANNY. You think I'm doing this for you? Listen, I'm just doing this so you'll realize what is obvious to the most casual passerby— that I am a staggeringly handsome man who is also your perfect and eternal soul mate, that I— *(She throws her arms around him and hugs him hard.)* —that I'm the one you want.

Ellen rises from the couch and crosses back into the present.

ELLEN. Where do you look for a blind spot? *(Beat.)* Do you know what just recently occurred to me? You've probably realized this before, but it just occurred to me that when people say they want change—what they really mean is—I want *you* to change. *(Beat.)* Because it's easy to see someone else's blind spot, isn't it? But it's... *Wow.* It's so much harder to see your own.

End of Act One

ACT TWO

Scene 1

PROJECTIONS: COVERAGE OF CONGRESS' VOTE TO AUTHORIZE BUSH TO GO TO WAR, AND HILLARY CLINTON SPEAKING ABOUT THE DIFFICULTY OF HER VOTE IN FAVOR OF AUTHORIZATION.

Early October 2002. Eight months later.

Ellen and Amy sit semi-dressed and cross-legged on the bed in Amy's Boston apartment, paging through their datebooks. They are infused with post-coital contentment and connection.

ELLEN.   I've got the first of those speaking gigs at Brown that Friday.
AMY.   Can I come and see you?
ELLEN.   Really?
AMY.   Can I?
ELLEN.   Of course. I would love that. *(Checking her calendar.)* Yes. Then I can come back with you and spend the weekend here. Is that okay? *(Amy nods. It's a happy plan. Ellen flirts.)* They're putting me in a hotel. *(Amy pushes Ellen down on the bed and straddles her, pinning her arms down.)*
AMY.   I love a hotel.
ELLEN.   *(Suddenly, charmingly, dissolved by desire.)* You do? *(Amy, still holding Ellen's arms down, kisses her deeply. Then she gets up and starts to dress, no agenda, just preparing for Ellen to leave. Ellen, still in a swoon and stupid with desire for Amy to come back and do more things to her, flops around on the bed.)*
AMY.   What's happening over there?
ELLEN.   *(Suddenly feeling exposed, embarrassed.)* I feel...
AMY.   What?
ELLEN.   *(She can hardly say it.)* I feel...needy.

AMY. *(Direct, and with easy, simple authority.)* There's a difference between neediness…and need. *(Ellen is all hers.)* Need is very sexy.

ELLEN. *(A puddle of limp goofiness.)* How do you just say those things to me??? Look at what you do to me! I'm all undone! How do you do that to me???

AMY. I'm very talented.

ELLEN. You're so talented. You're a really talented artist. Why are you all the way over there?

AMY. Because it's time for you to go.

ELLEN. No, it's not.

AMY. Isn't your train in an hour?

ELLEN. There's no train. I wish I didn't have to go.

AMY. *(Simply.)* Then stay. *(A beat.)* Sometimes I want to reach in and shake you. I'm so mad at you that you're not mine.

ELLEN. I know.

AMY. Sometimes I do.

ELLEN. I know. I'm walking down the street and I feel it.

AMY. Sometimes I find you and kiss you from the inside.

ELLEN. I know.

AMY. *(Rueful disbelief.)* A year and a half. *(Ellen nods.)* You're going to D.C. next week.

ELLEN. Yeah. *(A small beat, then Ellen begins to dress.)*

AMY. *(Normal, open tone.)* Are you going to see Judy?

ELLEN. Yeah. I'm just there for a night but I'll see her for dinner. I'll be glad to talk to her. I'm a little worried about Tessa. She's having a hard time and— *(Sees the tears coming down Amy's cheeks.)* No. No. What's happening? *(Amy shrugs it off.)* Amy, Amy, I'm sorry I have to go. I know this is so hard. *(Amy shrugs her off, gathering herself into herself.)*

ELLEN. Amy…?

AMY. *(Sharp.)* What? *(A small beat.)* Look, this is the situation I've put myself in. I have to deal with it.

ELLEN. With me.

AMY. No, not with you.

ELLEN. Of course with me.

AMY. No, Ellen. What do you think? You leave here and go back to your family.

ELLEN. I—Yes.

AMY. I would break you and Danny up if I thought that relationship wasn't worthy. I've broken up relationships. But what you have with him, and, all of it, Kayla and Laurie—If I had that I would never leave it. And you're not going to leave it. Are you?

ELLEN. I know. I know. But—

AMY. Ellen, I need someone of my own. *(Small beat.)*

ELLEN. *(True acknowledgment.)* I know. Amy, I know you do.

AMY. And... Then what's going to happen?

ELLEN. I—

AMY. You'll go away. I'll lose you.

ELLEN. No. No, Amy. That's wrong. If you found someone else I would feel—very bad, oh my god I can hardly even think about...how that would feel. *(About this she is very clear.)* But I would figure out how to stay in your life.

AMY. How?

ELLEN. I don't know. But I would.

AMY. I don't know how you'd be able to do that. I don't believe yc

ELLEN. I wouldn't have a choice! Amy, Amy, look, nothing ab this relationship is...easy or comfortable or...it's not a light party we're having here...but we're here because we're ch; each other. Amy, look at me. What happens to me you...*undone*...nothing but *feeling*... This is new. This is some-thing I couldn't even imagine before you. And I know how you let me hold your heart. *(Amy starts to cry.)* And I know no one has ever done that before. I feel it. I feel your heart. You're right, we can't stay in this configuration, certain things will have to change—but listen to me, *listen to me.* I will never not be holding your heart.

Scene 2

PROJECTIONS: COVERAGE OF CHENEY, BUSH, TONY BLAIR AND ROBERT BYRD, EACH TALKING ABOUT THE IMMINENT INVASION OF IRAQ.

February 15, 2003. Four months later. The day of global protest against the invasion of Iraq.

Danny, Ellen and Kayla have just returned from the march and are sprawled out in Danny and Ellen's apartment. The TV is on and Ellen flips through the channels. Laurie enters.

LAURIE. Hi, you guys.

DANNY Hey!   ELLEN. Hey, Laur.   KAYLA. Hi.

LAURIE. *(Kissing Kayla.)* Hey honey. How was it?

KAYLA. It was good. It was exciting. They're saying there were four hundred thousand people there. I'm tired!

DANNY. If I had the energy to reach forward I'd take my shoes off. My dogs are barkin'!

KAYLA. Oh, I know. *(Holding her feet out.)* Honey, help me! *(Laurie takes Kayla's shoes off and rubs her feet.)*

ELLEN. *(Still on the TV.)* Unbelievable! It was fucking huge and there's virtually no coverage!

LAURIE. I saw it on CNN.

ELLEN. Yes, they mention that a protest took place. But it's the biggest protest in world history! The only place there weren't protests was in mainland China. Why isn't it the fucking lead? Well, we did get slightly more coverage than the Valentine's Day thieves who stole thousands of roses. That was an important story! *(Clicks off the TV, disgusted.)* God! Why is everybody so fucking *stupid?*

KAYLA. *(Weary laugh.)* Oh, Ellen…

ELLEN. What? *(Beat.)* What?

KAYLA. Nothing. *(Ellen waits.)* You know, there are some serious people who are saying this invasion is a good idea.

ELLEN. Whaaaatt?

KAYLA. I'm not saying I agree with them, but we can't just dismiss them out of hand.

ELLEN. Like who?

KAYLA. Oh...Ellen, you know.

LAURIE. Gephardt.

KAYLA. Gephardt.

DANNY. Bonus points, Laurie. Have you been watching *Face the Nation* again?

LAURIE. Danny, you know my show is *Meet The Press.*

ELLEN. Gephardt? Laurie, Al Gore was too conservative for you.

LAURIE. I'm just winning my bonus points.

KAYLA. What about the *New York Times* editorial // page?

ELLEN. AAAHHH. The fucking *New York Times* editorial page!

KAYLA. Thomas Friedman is making some // interesting arguments, Ellen.

DANNY. *(Mock horror.)* Oh, no, not Tom Friedman!

ELLEN. Tom Friedman can bite my ass.

KAYLA. Well, he is an expert in the region. // He says getting rid of Saddam could transform the region.

ELLEN. Oh. Tom Friedman has lost his marbles. Tom Friedman is a crazed Pollyanna. What he says would make sense except that they're proposing to initiate this transformation by bombing the hell out of the place.

KAYLA. Alright then, Tony Blair.

ELLEN. I know, I can't figure that one out.

KAYLA. He's not a stupid man.

DANNY. *(Mock amazement.)* That's what I was gonna say.

KAYLA. It is possible they know something we don't know. *(Off Ellen's reaction.)* It is.

ELLEN. Look, obviously Saddam is terrible. But their solution is...to blow the place up? *(Others speak underneath Ellen's rant.)*

ELLEN. What do they think is going to happen? Do they really believe democracy magically emerges from chaos? You know what? They do. They do. These are guys who actually believe that everything thing about their wealthy, insulated lives is a result of their personal hard	LAURIE. Who wants beer? DANNY. Oh, me. KAYLA. Ooh yeah. *(A beat as Laurie goes to the kitchen, gets the beers and passes them out.)* DANNY. Ah. Thanks.

work. Listen to them talk. It's astonishing. George Bush actually believes he earned his inherited wealth. Bush, Cheney, Rumsfeld, that comb-over weasel Wolfowitz, they're fantasists!!

LAURIE. *(To Kayla.)* Here you go, honey.
KAYLA. Oh…thank you, honey.
DANNY. *(Toasts, then drinks.)* Ah, that's good.
LAURIE. *(Holding a beer out to Ellen. A beat.)* Do you want this?

(Taking the beer from Laurie.)
Thanks. A pre-emptive war?! What the fuck is that? The only reason that can make sense to them is that they don't know the slightest thing about actual war.
KAYLA. Unlike you?
ELLEN. Of course, I don't know anything about war. But I'm reasonably sure that it's the height of arrogance to think that you can attack a country and be able to control the outcome. Are you really agreeing with Tom Friedman?
KAYLA. No, Ellen. But I… I…
LAURIE. Honey?
KAYLA. *(Still trying.)* Just… I just…
LAURIE. Honey? Let it go.
ELLEN. *(Seeing their communication.)* What?
LAURIE. *(Still to Kayla.)* It's not worth it.
ELLEN. Laurie, what's going on?
LAURIE. *(Friendly, brushing it off.)* It's okay.
DANNY. What are you ladies up to tonight? And by ladies I mean big-rig driving, strap-on wearing—
KAYLA. *(A warning.)* Daniel?
DANNY. You know…ladies.
KAYLA. Oh. I don't know. Honey, are you cooking tonight or—
LAURIE. I don't feel like it. Can we go out?
KAYLA. Sure, of course. *(Realizing they haven't asked the others.)* Do you guys feel like going out for dinner tonight?
DANNY. Sure.
KAYLA. Oh, good.
DANNY. I mean… I can go. *(To Ellen.)* I don't know when you're…
ELLEN. Oh, I want to go! Oh man, I'd love to go out with you guys tonight. I have to—I have to go out of town and I have to leave late tonight.
KAYLA. *(Excited.)* Oh, is this the week you're going to the Aspen Institute?

ELLEN. No. No, that's next week. No, *(Keeping the tone light and even.)* I'm going to Boston.

KAYLA. *(Also carefully light and even.)* Oh.

LAURIE. Oh.

KAYLA. That's too bad.

ELLEN. I know. Can we make a plan for the week after next?

KAYLA. *(Eager.)* Yeah, we should *definitely* make a plan now because... or... Yeah. Good idea.

ELLEN. What's up?

KAYLA. Uh—

LAURIE. You can tell them now, it's fine with me.

ELLEN. Tell us what? *(Slight beat.)*

KAYLA. It's... God, such a big build-up now! It's not that big of a deal... It's just... I'm considering going back to school. *(A slight beat.)*

ELLEN. You are?

DANNY. Okay. Finally getting your G.E.D. It's about time.

KAYLA. Our director of donor relations is about to leave and they'd like to hire me for the job but they can't because I don't have a Master's. And, well, it got me thinking, you know, it might be a good idea to get a Master's, I mean I won't get that job, of course, but I'd kind of like the option to move up somewhere at some point and... Yeah... So...

ELLEN. So...what kind degree would you get?

KAYLA. It'd be a Master's in Organizational Management.

ELLEN. Huh.

KAYLA. Yeah. I looked at a lot of programs. I was accepted to one.

LAURIE. *(Proud of her.)* Well, you were accepted to three.

KAYLA. Yeah, but I was accepted to one that's interesting to me.

ELLEN. Where?

KAYLA. Uh...Madison.

ELLEN. Madison?

DANNY. Huh. Sounds like a plan.

ELLEN. Is it a plan?

KAYLA. It might be.

ELLEN. Are you guys moving to Wisconsin?

KAYLA. We might be.

LAURIE. Yes.

KAYLA. Yes.

ELLEN. Oh. That's...big.

KAYLA. Things change, you know, Ellen. Things shift. We're just, well, in a way, we're just catching up with that.

LAURIE. We really do want to have a kid.

KAYLA. Yeah, and that's not something that just happens—

DANNY. Not for the lesbians.

KAYLA. —and…you know, Laurie's put up with the tenement living long enough. And…also…it doesn't feel the same as it used to. You know? It doesn't have the same romance it did—back in our heyday. *(Small beat.)*

DANNY. Well, all I can say is that I am going to miss the // hell out of…

KAYLA. Okay, calm down, we're not leaving immediately. // We just wanted you to—

DANNY. No, you didn't let me finish. I'm going to miss the hell out of Laurie! *(He wraps Laurie in a huge bear hug.)* // Goddammit, I'm gonna miss you! You're like the brother I never had!

LAURIE. Shut. Up.

KAYLA. Oh my god, you are a butt pain! *(A beat.)* Ellen? Speak.

ELLEN. I think it's great, Kayla.

DANNY. Good job, Sister.

ELLEN. I think it's really smart.

KAYLA. Thanks.

ELLEN. Oh. Oh. You know what I keep meaning to ask you? Did you get that email I sent from that woman?

KAYLA. What email?

ELLEN. She has a small publishing house? *(Ellen goes to her computer to look for the email.)*

KAYLA. Oh. Oh. That's okay, // Ellen.

ELLEN. No. Shoot. I meant to check with you again about it. She's putting together an anthology, and I wanted you to send her your stuff…

KAYLA. Ellen, it's… // really…

ELLEN. *(Continuing to look.)* No, it's okay. I'm sure the email is still here…

KAYLA. Ellen, stop.

ELLEN. *(Undeterred.)* No, but… Oh Kayla, seriously, she'd love // your work. Where did I *put* that—

KAYLA. Ellen, stop it! Stop. Ellen. I'm not a writer any more!

ELLEN. *(Beat.)* Of course you are.

KAYLA. No. I've let that go.

ELLEN. For a while. Because you've been concentrating on other things.

KAYLA. Ellen, I can't operate that way. It makes me feel like a failure.

ELLEN. What way?

KAYLA. In a constantly...liminal state...

ELLEN. But that's not // the only way to...

KAYLA. Look, you've figured out how to make it work. I admire it. Truthfully, it makes me so jealous. But I can't do what you do. You thrive on constant flux. To me that is unbearable. I accept who I am and I'm making conscious choices and I want you to stop judging them.

ELLEN. I don't judge // your choices but—

KAYLA. Or not—but accept them! I need you to accept them because they're painful enough.

ELLEN. You're just—you're such—You're not someone who's supposed to walk away from your gift, from your talent //—there are so many ways to—

KAYLA. I miss thinking of myself as writer, Ellen. I miss thinking of myself as a person who's going to make that kind of impact in the world. But I've come to realize that, unlike you, I need to know, roughly, what my days are going to be like. I need to know there's going to be some money in the bank, I need a nice place to come home to, I need to come home and find my love there and I need to know it's not going to change on a daily basis. I need that more than I need to be a writer. I can't do anything about the fact that that seems small to you. *(Kayla and Ellen share a long look. Ellen nods.)*

ELLEN. Okay.

KAYLA. Okay. *(A long beat.)*

LAURIE. We're going to be back, eventually.

ELLEN. I don't know, Laurie. I think you might really like suburban living.

LAURIE. Yes, I will. But Kayla's going to be, like, "Midwesterners, talk faster!" *(A beat.)* Listen, in two years we're probably all going to be living together in Houston.

ELLEN. Okay, if that's your plan to make me feel better about Madison, it might actually be working.

KAYLA. Houston! How did you come up with Houston? We are never moving to Houston!

DANNY. Now you've gone too far. Even for me. Houston? That's fucked up.

LAURIE. I don't know! I'm just… I don't know! Don't make fun of me!

ELLEN. Oh, we weren't. KAYLA. Sorry. Oh, we're not, honey, we're not! DANNY. We're not.

LAURIE. *(Overlapping them, wanting them to stop.)* It's fine. I'm totally fine. Everything is fine. Everything is fine. I'm going to go down. *(Getting up to leave. To Danny.)* So we're seeing you later tonight, right?

DANNY. Abso-freakin-lutely.

LAURIE. Super. Okay. *(To Kayla.)* You have anything for the laundry besides what's in the hamper?

KAYLA. *(Getting up.)* Yeah. I'm coming with you. *(To Ellen and Danny.)* Okay, so we will make a date for—two weeks from now?

ELLEN. Yeah, 'cause next week I'm // in Aspen.

KAYLA. Oh, that's when you're at Aspen, right. That's going to be really great, Ellen.

ELLEN. Yeah, I think so. Thanks.

KAYLA. So we'll have dinner in two weeks. And Danny, what time tonight?

DANNY. I'm a free agent.

KAYLA. Okay, we'll call you in a little while. *(They leave. Ellen and Danny each straighten the room in silence for a few beats.)*

ELLEN. I feel kind of sad.

DANNY. Yeah.

ELLEN. Did you have any idea that was happening?

DANNY. No. I mean, Kayla's been talking off and on about going back to school, but I didn't know she was actually applying to places.

ELLEN. Wanna try to stop 'em?

DANNY. I don't think we can do that.

ELLEN. I guess not.

DANNY. I don't think so.

ELLEN. It's a lot to take in. *(A beat.)*

DANNY. So, what's up with you these days, Ellie?

ELLEN. In what way?

DANNY. In the way of what's up with you these days, Ellie?

ELLEN. I don't know. Kind of status quo. I don't know.

DANNY. I think it's time for you to make a choice. *(The ground gives way beneath Ellen. She can't find words for an unbearably long time. Then—she describes the only image in her head—)*

64

ELLEN. I keep seeing your face, Danny, when you got off that bus, the time you came to see me in Vermont.

DANNY. Oh, yeah.

ELLEN. I don't even remember what that place was called. "The Center for Progressive…Something," I don't know, it was such a miserable place, I'd been there two months writing grants. It was the first year we were together. *(Danny nods.)* And you came to see me.

DANNY. Yeah.

ELLEN. Yeah.

DANNY. It would have been a seven-hour drive. That bus took eighteen hours.

ELLEN. I know. It was, like, one-thirty in the morning. *(A marvel.)* You came all that way.

DANNY. Yeah.

ELLEN. And I'll never forget your face, Danny, getting off that bus…with your hoodie sweatshirt under that tweed coat I hated from the Goodwill and the hood pulled up and tied under your chin.

DANNY. It was…cold.

ELLEN. *(Looking into the beloved face she is describing.)* Your face… Even when I think if it now, it kills me. How much love there was in that face. I saw you and I burst into tears. That face, that sweet open face with your love for me on it, so…open, so clear. And I thought—I thought—No one will ever love me this cleanly, this clearly again.

DANNY. That's true.

ELLEN. I know.

DANNY. You have to choose, Ellie. You don't have to choose me. But you have to choose.

Scene 3

PROJECTIONS: COVERAGE OF BUSH ADMINIS-
TRATION OFFICIALS' COMMENTARY ON THE
PROGRESS OF THE IRAQ INVASION.

Mid-March 2003. A month later.

Amy's apartment in Boston, Amy sits on the bed. Ellen watch-
es her.

ELLEN. Amy? Amy?

AMY. What?

ELLEN. Say something.

AMY. What?

ELLEN. I don't know. What are you // feeling?

AMY. I saw it coming! I saw it coming! What is there to say about it? I knew this is what was going to happen.

ELLEN. Amy, it's going to be okay.

AMY. For you! You're fine! You have Danny and Kayla and Laurie and your whole family, and they're so funny and loving and all your // plans and your—

ELLEN. I'm not choosing them over you, Amy.

AMY. You are! Don't—I can't stand to listen to you tell me that. Why did I ever listen to you?

ELLEN. *(Fierce, honest.)* You listened to me because I was saying things that were true, and they're still true. We can't be lovers— *(Amy collapses.)* but it will be okay. Amy, I'm telling you this even though it's going to kill me when you fall in love with somebody else.

AMY. I will. I will find someone else.

ELLEN. I know you will.

AMY. No, I don't want it! I don't want anyone else. *(Small beat.)* *Why is it you?* Every relationship before you, I'd be okay for a few weeks and then I'd just want out. But I'd think, this relationship is fine. It's me who's wrong. And I'd try so hard and it would end so badly. And so I knew it was me. And so I knew I'd always be alone.

But my...heart... My heart...was calm with you. And it imagined being with you for a very long time. Why is that? Why did I get the thing I couldn't imagine with you?

ELLEN. Amy, it's going to kill me not to be close to you like this anymore. *(They are merged in their grief.)*

AMY. I know.

ELLEN. Feel this! We can practically hold it in our hands, this feeling between us, my god, my god it's so heavy, it's, its in us.

AMY. No, I don't want it.

ELLEN. Amy... There's love. And there's desire. But this is something... Older. Bigger. More. I don't even believe in things like what I'm trying to describe. But that's what this is. That's why this feeling; this has always been here between us. We don't get to be lovers. *(Amy collapses, sobbing.)* I know. It's unbearable. But we will be something else. I don't know what that's going to be, but this doesn't go away. It won't go away, it will just be different. It will transform into something else. It will, Amy. It will.

Ellen steps away from Amy and back into the present.

ELLEN. How do we know when the worst is over? You know that saying? Until you hit the ground, falling can feel remarkably like flying.

Scene 4

PROJECTIONS: FRAGMENTS OF THE SECOND BUSH-KERRY DEBATE.

October 2004. A year and a half later.

Ellen calls Amy from a hotel room in Ohio.

AMY. *(Brightly.)* Hey.

ELLEN. Hey there. I'm so, so sorry I haven't called. I'm in Ohio. I've been here since last Tuesday.

AMY. That's okay. How's it going?

ELLEN. Oh God! Ken Blackwell, the secretary of state—right-wing Republican—says voter registration cards will be considered invalid unless they're printed on 80-pound paper.

AMY. That's terrible!

ELLEN. Oh, it's...shameless! How are you? *(Small beat.)*

AMY. Good.

ELLEN. You sound good.

AMY. I am.

ELLEN. I haven't heard your voice sound like this in a long time. What's going on?

AMY. Do you really want to know?

ELLEN. *(A fraction of a beat.)* Yeah.

AMY. I've met someone.

ELLEN. *(And the ground is gone. And she is falling, falling, falling.)* Oh.

AMY. I like her. And she likes me, too. I can tell.

ELLEN. Oh.

AMY. Are you okay?

ELLEN. *(Sits on the bed. Can't hold herself up.)* Yeah. I'm... Yeah. That's good. *(She endeavors to keep her voice positive and engaged, even though she is literally collapsing.)* That's so good, Amy. What's her name?

AMY. Anne.

ELLEN. Where did you meet her?

AMY. One of her friends set us up.

ELLEN. Oh. Oh. What does she do?

AMY. She works at a pre-school. She's…assistant administrator is her title. She kind of runs the office there.

ELLEN. Oh. That sounds really nice.

AMY. She's… She's a single mom. Tween…tweens…tweenagers, they call them. Twelve and thirteen. They're not—not too sure how they feel about me.

ELLEN. Oh. That's, um… That's um…

AMY. Are you okay?

ELLEN. Yeah. I'm… I'm…*(Sobbing. Not letting Amy hear her.)*

AMY. Ellen.

ELLEN. Yeah?

AMY. You have to stick with me here. It's going to be okay.

ELLEN. *(As brightly as she can.)* I know. I know.

AMY. I had to find someone, Ellen.

ELLEN. I know, I know, Amy, I know, I know.

AMY. When are you coming back? When can I see you?

ELLEN. I don't—I don't—I will, but… I can't…right now… I don't know.

AMY. Ellen, I need to see you. When you see me you'll know it's fine.

ELLEN. No, I know. I just can't right now. I'm really okay. You have to just let me take it in. I just need—I'll call you when I can.

AMY. When will that be?

ELLEN. I… I don't know.

Scene 5

*PROJECTIONS: COVERAGE OF BUSH'S VICTORY
WITH MORE POPULAR VOTES THAN ANY PRESI-
DENTIAL CANDIDATE IN HISTORY.*

November 2004. Four days after the election.

Judy and Ellen sit in Ellen's living room.

ELLEN. Oh, Judy. I liked having you close. I don't want you to leave. It's so soon. Next week?

JUDY. Yeah. That might actually be why I took the job. I'll be far away for Thanksgiving. I hate that fucking holiday.

ELLEN. This is a particularly bad one, huh?

JUDY. I can't say I didn't see what was coming with Larry.

ELLEN. Sucks, though. We're driving out to Wisconsin for Thanksgiving.

JUDY. Why are you driving?

ELLEN. There's some big ball of twine out there that Danny wants to see. He's very excited about it. *(Beat.)* It's so hard on him. The way I am right now. I'm fine and then I just... I just... I can't get a hold of myself. It's horrible. I try to keep it together and not—god!—make him have to deal with my feelings about her. *(A beat.)* I knew that it would be hard but I thought I could make myself...big enough to deal with what would happen. But I feel...ruined. That's the word that keeps coming into my head—ruined.

JUDY. I'm so sorry, honey.

ELLEN. *(Shaking it off.)* Ach! I'm okay. *(Turning her attention to her friend, taking her in.)* Judy, I'm so upset about Tessa.

JUDY. Yes.

ELLEN. I'm still...not clear about what happened.

JUDY. As far as I can tell, somebody at the school told her they needed records from her school in Kentucky or she was going to lose her financial aid. She asked Eileen, who... *(Waves it off, no point getting into all the ways Eileen didn't follow through.)* And her old school didn't have her records…they lost them. She couldn't get the papers she was told she needed. So she left.

ELLEN. Why?

JUDY. She thought they were throwing her out.

ELLEN. But they weren't, were they?

JUDY. An administrator there told her that without that paperwork she would lose her financial aid.

ELLEN. And…did // you—

JUDY. *(With increasing impatience.)* I wrote to her school. I wrote to Kentucky social services. I assumed it was being taken care of.

ELLEN. Oh God, it's unbelievable she's back in Corbin. It's so crazy! We could have pulled strings // for her

JUDY. She didn't know that.

ELLEN. No, no, I get it, I get it. I just… I know D.C. was so hard for her at first but I thought she had really…risen above it.

JUDY. She was never not having a hard time.

ELLEN. Yeah. Well, she has to come back to D.C.

JUDY. To what?

ELLEN. Oh I… I don't know. I was thinking if she got a job— But I know you're leaving—

JUDY. *(Finally snaps.)* What kind of job would she get with no high school diploma that would make her enough money to live there? *(Ellen nods. A beat.)*

JUDY. I can't do it again, Ellen.

ELLEN. I know. *(A beat.)* Well, at least the election went well.

JUDY. *(A laugh.)* Oh yeah.

ELLEN. I don't know, Judy. I don't know. I woke up in that horrible hotel room in Ohio on Wednesday morning and I couldn't—I couldn't turn on the TV. I couldn't bear to hear them say that he had won again. I felt so sick.

JUDY. It's sickening.

ELLEN. My roommate, this woman who'd traveled from Arizona to help get people to the polls, she and I just lay there. Nobody could talk. I don't think I've ever felt people so crushed politically. So many people worked so fucking hard. How did it happen? I mean when you went to the polls, how many people were in line?

JUDY. I didn't vote. *(Beat.)*

ELLEN. What?

JUDY. I don't vote.

ELLEN. I don't… I can't… How could you not vote in this election? How could you—help George Bush to get re-elected?

JUDY. I didn't do that.

ELLEN. You didn't vote. I don't understand. I don't know how you, especially—You're out there seeing first-hand the impact he's having in the world, how could you not have cast a vote against him?

JUDY. I don't vote.

ELLEN. Never?

JUDY. No.

ELLEN. Okay. You have to say more

JUDY. I—I don't want to participate in a system I don't believe in.

ELLEN. What system? The American system?

JUDY. Right.

ELLEN. *(Not believing Judy is seriously making this argument.)* You don't believe in American democracy?

JUDY. No.

ELLEN. *(Incredulous.)* You don't believe in American democracy.

JUDY. No.

ELLEN. *(Dumbfounded.)* That's crazy.

JUDY. Why?

ELLEN. What system is better?

JUDY. I don't know. But I do know that voting is a false exercise. You know this. You're the one who talks about how the system is skewed so that the votes in rich, white Republican districts are counted at much higher levels.

ELLEN. If more people voted they could change that.

JUDY. How? Gore did get more votes than Bush.

ELLEN. I know, but—

JUDY. The Supreme Court handed Bush the election.

ELLEN. Yes, exactly. This right-wing mob has abdicated from the system. That's why we have to do everything we can to get them out before they dismantle the whole apparatus.

JUDY. *(Obvious.)* The apparatus is working as it's meant to work, to facilitate the self interests of wealthy men in power.

ELLEN. But that's not what it's meant to do.

JUDY. Ellen, for the first twenty-something years of this country only white male property owners could vote. That's what this country was set up to do. We can put whatever Band-Aids on that we want, but that's the set-up.

ELLEN. Okay, yes. The founders reflected the world at the time. But they set up systems that could grow and become more inclusive.

JUDY. I think you have a totally romanticized view of their intentions and of any inclusion. My grandmother grew up in a world where she couldn't vote. The Voting Rights Act wasn't passed until 1965. When *I* was in junior high school, black people still couldn't vote.

[Note: Ellen is not defensive with Judy. She knows much of what Judy says makes sense. But she also knows there's a counter-argument to be made that can hold both Judy's reality and her own belief in American democracy. Throughout this scene she's trying to find it. As for Judy, her arguments are not driven by disillusionment and rage, but rather an almost bemused disbelief that Ellen cannot see what to Judy is as plain as day.]

ELLEN. Okay. Yes. Maybe I'm assigning retroactive intentionality. That's probably right. That's what we do, right? We look back at things that happened randomly and we assign intentionality to them. But that's what I'm saying. The genius of the system is that it was set up to allow for the dynamic accretion of those random events which have made the system more inclusive.

JUDY. Whatever inclusion you see has happened in spite of the system, not because of it.

ELLEN. What about Civil Rights? The judicial branch stepped up and the system protected the minority, as it was meant to.

JUDY. Are you talking about the Supreme Court?

ELLEN. Yes.

JUDY. The Supreme Court that said that Dred Scott was not a citizen and could never be one because he was black? The Supreme Court that defended the // Japanese internment camps—

ELLEN. Alright. Alright. But as more people, more women and more minorities have gotten power, those things shift.

JUDY. Where do you see that manifesting?

ELLEN. Everywhere.

JUDY. Look, Ellen, the idea that the system leads to a place for everyone is a myth. There has never been a place for everyone. It's only the people who benefit from that who think there is. But the people at the top are the same people who've always been at the top. And the people who are at the bottom are the same people who've always been at the bottom.

ELLEN. But // —

JUDY. But what, Ellen? I see a system that adjusts to maintain that order. Occasionally, a door cracks open for a decade or so, and then it gets slammed shut. Reconstruction lasted twenty years and was crushed by Jim Crow. Johnson's War on Poverty was actually working. You know that, right? Nixon put Rumsfeld and Cheney in charge of it and told them to strangle it. It's all documented. It's no secret. Poor people aren't even part of the political discussion any more. Have you noticed that? What I see in the wake of Civil Rights is the population of black men exploding in prison. I see less access to health care, to public schools, to all sorts of public amenities. All the things you rail about. It's not coincidental that those things are being privatized, being put into the hands of fewer people with more money and taken out of the public sector. Poor people and black people are suffering and that's not an anomaly. That's written into the system.

ELLEN. But Judy, change is possible here. People can move. Isn't that what you did? Aren't you the example of that.

JUDY. No. I'm an exception that proves the rule. I had a tremendous amount of luck. People who crossed my path, teachers and so forth who pulled me onto a different track.

ELLEN. But isn't that the thing? Isn't that the system?

JUDY. No. That's luck. Plus I was smart.

ELLEN. Right.

JUDY. Yes. If you're poor and you're smart you might get out. Rich people don't have to be smart. Middle-class people don't either.

ELLEN. *(Really trying to understand.)* So what are you saying? There's no special potential in our system? It's not any better for poor people here than—what? A refugee camp in Guinea? Saddam Hussein's Iraq?

JUDY. Yes, I'm saying that for some people there is no more potential here.

ELLEN. I don't see that.

JUDY. Right. Because you're a middle-class person and you are served well by the system, so you have to believe that change is possible. It's what American liberals do. Because what could you do otherwise? You'd have to give up your middle-class life or your ideals.

ELLEN. No. No. The difference here is aspirational. Not everyone is treated the same here, of course. But it is the goal. There is an equality of aspiration.

JUDY. But that's what I'm saying. There's not. Look at my sister, staying with a man who beats her. Look at my mother, sabotaging herself and her kid at every turn. You know that stereotype of welfare dependency the right wing loves talk about? That's my family. Do I look at them and think they're fuck-ups? Yes. Do I blame them for the fact that Tessa couldn't keep it together long enough to just get a lousy high school diploma? Yes. That girl broke my fucking heart. I'm ashamed of my family. It's unbearable to me. I can hardly even get the words out of my mouth because I'm ashamed of being ashamed. The political line on them is they just aren't trying hard enough. They don't believe in themselves. And it's true. And why? Because they don't have that sense of *aspiration* you're talking about. Because they live in an America where, if you can't get the paperwork you're told you need for the forms someone tells you you have to fill out, you are shit out of luck. They live in an America that is configured to keep them right where they are. And if you grow up in that place, you understand that—and if you don't, you don't.

ELLEN. Okay…but—flawed as it is—it is the system that gives the best quality of life to the biggest number of people.

JUDY. *(Rueful laugh.)* Okay, Ellen. First of all, you know that's not true. Look at health care. And education. And whatever else—it's just not true. Second—isn't this the thing you rail against? The blind assumption that this country is good, even when it's behaving badly? Isn't this what you want? To find the blind spots, look at what's really happening and to go deeper?

ELLEN. Yes.

JUDY. You talk about what people take for granted—you take for granted your own worth—you take for granted that you are worthy of love. Who but someone who completely believes in that could live the way you've lived? Who else could make the choices you've made? You can criticize marriage and have "expansive" thoughts about relationships, not because you think the system of marriage is wrong, but because you don't need it. You don't need to be reassured you won't be left. Most people, they don't know that. They don't believe that. Look at how shocked you are. How can that be the case? How did you get this far in life without having your heart broken?

ELLEN. I don't know.

Ellen steps back into the present.

ELLEN. *(Dawning.)* I don't know why I thought... I mean, it's obvious, it's obvious, it's obvious. The thing about the blind spot— is...*you can't see it.* It doesn't matter how much you try...*that's what makes it a blind spot. (A beat.)* So... So... What? What can you do? *(A beat.)* Look at your wake, I guess—at the damage you've left in your wake... And try to figure out what was really happening when you were looking forward, trying so hard, thinking you were paying such close, careful attention.

Scene 6

PROJECTIONS: FRAGMENTED IMAGES OF KATRINA AND ITS AFTERMATH

September 2005. Ten months later.

Danny and Ellen are in their living room, getting ready to go to the beach. Danny is singing a happy, meander-y going-to-the-beach song he's making up as he goes along.

DANNY. *(Sings.) Going to the beach. We're going to the beach. What's more fun than the beach—*
ELLEN. *(Holding the sunscreen.)* Did you get the tops of your ears?
DANNY. Yep—*There's sand and sun and a big roller coaster—*
ELLEN. Did you get the tops of your feet?
DANNY. Yep—*and some washed up syringes and some other kinds of trash at the New York Beach! Love the beach! I love the beach!* Hey! We're going to the beach! *(Ellen points to a plastic grocery bag. He picks it up.)* What is this?
ELLEN. I cut up watermelon.
DANNY. Ah! Good thinkin', Linkin'.

ELLEN. It's the beach. You've gotta have watermelon and you gotta have your unread *New Yorker*s.

DANNY. Spoken like a true outdoorswoman. *(She ties a sweater around her waist and picks up an overflowing tote bag and a plastic grocery bag with more stuff in it. Danny picks up another plastic grocery bag and two folded beach chairs he's rigged with belts to be carried like a backpack.)* Ready. Ready?

ELLEN. Yeah. *(She looks for her keys.)* Where'd my keys go? They were here. *(Danny looks too.)* They were right here. Where'd they go?

DANNY. Don't know. I have my mine.

ELLEN. I know but— *(Continuing to look with increasing frustration.)* obviously, I need my keys. Would you go out without your own keys?

DANNY. Well, they've gotta be here somewhere.

ELLEN. They were right here! They were right here!

DANNY. Well... I...

ELLEN. No, I know, Danny! I— *(Suddenly she is sobbing. Overcome.)* Sorry.

DANNY. *(Suddenly so weary.)* Oh. Ellie... *(He gets the Kleenex box and puts it next to her.)*

ELLEN. *(Struggling to get a hold of herself.)* No. No. No. No. No. I'm fine. I'm fine. I'm fine. *(For a moment getting control.)* Okay. I'm good. I'm good. I'm sorry. I'm sorry about that. I'm totally fine. Just... *(Starting to lose it again.)* let me get a drink of water. *(She goes to the kitchen to drink some water. She returns, cheerfully ready to go.)* Okay. Let's go. *(She picks up her bag and heads for the door. Danny gathers his things to follow her. She is again overcome. Danny waits. Ellen, sobbing, face in hands, speaks to herself.)* Oh my god. I want to just go to sleep and wake up in ten years. *(Danny unceremoniously drops the bags and the chairs and begins to put things away.)* What are you doing?

DANNY. Putting these away.

ELLEN. No! Danny! We're going. I'm fine. I'm totally fine. Come on, come on, come on, come on, let's go. I'm so fine.

DANNY. You're not.

ELLEN. I really want to go. I really do. Come on. Once we're at the beach, we'll feel so much better.

DANNY. I'm going out for a walk.

ELLEN. No. Danny?

DANNY. Ellen, I'll just go take a walk and you...do what you need to do and...we'll go to the beach another time.

ELLEN. Danny, wait. *(He stops, looks at her. Waits.)* I know it's horrible that I'm like this. *(Danny nearly laughs at the understatement.)* No, I know, Danny… I know. But I'm getting through it. I'm trying to get through it.

DANNY. What do you want me to say? This isn't about me. You're crying over your keys!

ELLEN. I know—but it's going to get better. I swear.

DANNY. But—You're not here.

ELLEN. I am. I'm right here.

DANNY. No. You're not…in this…relationship.

ELLEN. Of course I am.

DANNY. Not… Not… Not in the way I am.

ELLEN. Danny, that's not true.

DANNY. Everything I do… in my daily life…my, my…long-term and short-term …I don't know. Thinking? Planning? *All* of it is based on my assumption that we're …making a life together — But you don't do that! You don't have that assumption.
    ELLEN. Yes… Yes.

ELLEN. I…do.

DANNY. No. You want to be out on your own, and you like having me as your support system, but you're on your own, and you're willing to let me me writhe, Ellen, let everybody around you writhe while you go out into the world, pushing boundaries, taking what you want.
    ELLEN. No. That's not what I—

    ELLEN. Danny, that's not fair!

ELLEN. Okay, I know I push toward the thing I want—but you have to push me back. I do listen and I do want to know what you need and you know that that's true. But you have to tell me.

DANNY. *(Incredulous.)* I did.

ELLEN. *(Puzzled for a second—then—)* And…I chose to be with you. I am in this relationship, Danny. I think about it all the time! I…I do things for you… For us.… I planned this—tried to plan this whole…trip to the… Oh my god, it sounds so lame, so stupid. But every day… *I did choose you.*

DANNY. Choosing me doesn't mean just being here in this room!

ELLEN. That's not all I'm doing, Danny, that's not fair. Listen, if we want a life that's big and complicated // then—

DANNY. That's what *you* want.

ELLEN. You do too. That's why you're with me, Danny. Look—this moment is hard. But we have to just keep moving forward. We can't undo the choices we've made over these past years—we wouldn't want to. We're going to find our equilibrium again—

DANNY. When? *(He waits. Ellen has no response.)* Why am I waiting? There's always going to be something new pulling you away.

ELLEN. No—

DANNY. Yes! Because you want everything!

ELLEN. I... Yes.

DANNY. You can't choose me and have everything! That's not choosing!

ELLEN. *(Struggling to understand, to keep up, scared.)* That's not what I... That's not how I...

DANNY. *(Suddenly he understands—the fight is done.)* Ellen...I know you love me.

ELLEN. I do love you! I love you so much!

DANNY. I know. God, it... It fucking kills me... I've been waiting a long time—

ELLEN. No, Danny—

DANNY. —because I love you too
and I really...I really think I'm the
one you should be with. But it   ELLEN. You are!
doesn't matter now because, we're   Danny, you are!
now because, we're somewhere—
I don't know where—But things
are...different.

ELLEN. *(Terrified. Unprepared.)* Danny...?

DANNY. I...have to go out. I'm going for a walk. We'll talk...when I get back.

ELLEN. Okay. *(Danny leaves.)*

Scene 7

Ellen steps back into the present, with Judy.

ELLEN. So…I've been working… And that's good. I'm busy. It's good. *(A beat.)* I miss Danny.

JUDY. I know.

ELLEN. I feel like I can handle this as long as I feel like it's going to change, but I can't do this indefinitely. I keep waiting for things to turn, to shift—but what if it doesn't change? What if all I feel is loss? Oh, Judy, how much further do I have to fall? *(A beat or two.)*

JUDY. When I work in the camps, my job, as protection officer, is to try to make sure people aren't being denied access to food, water, shelter, medical aid because they're women or because they're from ethnic minority X or Y. My job is to try to make things a little more fair. That's all. Sometimes it works, sometimes it doesn't. I think the reason I keep going back is because these are places where no one thinks fairness is the natural way of things. The people I work with are desperate for fairness, for stability. But none of them believe it's a default setting that is automatically reverted // to.

ELLEN. I know these // things—

JUDY. Wait. *(A beat.)* I know that my refusal to have…hope…is damaging. It hurts me. It hurts people around me. I do know that. But I don't know how to let go of my rage. The American assumption that things always work out for the best—it's a willful blindness I cannot understand. I know you know these things, Ellen. But your question—how much further do I have to fall? That's an American question. It's the question of someone who has never really assumed she would fall at all.

Judy exits. Ellen, on the precipice of the void, speaks to herself and to us trying to work out—what happened?

ELLEN. The blind spot is right here. I know that it's here. And everyone can see it. But I can't see it, I can't see it, I can't see it. All I know is that all the things that worked for me for so long—my way of moving through the world—failed me. I wanted to be brave. I wanted not to be scared of change or disruption. I wanted to be brave enough to risk what I knew to walk toward what I didn't know. I wanted to feel more, know more, have more demanded of me, I wanted to love…more. I wanted more connection, more intimacy, more family… I thought if I could make myself brave enough to stand in an unknown place long enough…walls would shift, doors would open, a new way would show itself… *(A beat. A bone-deep realization.)* What…did I think risk *was*? What did I think it *was*? How is it that I built my life around an idea of "risk"—but never, never imagined I could lose the things most precious to me? *(A beat. A realization.)* I thought I was golden. I thought I was limitless. But now… *(Talking herself through her fear.)* This is where I live This is where I live now. I'm afraid. This is where I live. I don't know this place. I'm afraid. But this is where I live. *(Willing herself to be brave enough, Ellen steps into the negative space.)* Look. Look at your life. What is here? What do you see here? *(She allows herself to apprehend the fathomless emptiness before her. And then:)* Nothing. In the dizzying grief I feel for my family…I can see…the shape of my love. I can see, from here, the pulsing, bursting beauty of it. In this keening, aching loss I feel…I see the shape of my desire. Oh! I can see it from here. I said I wanted more… *(Beginning, finally, to see.)* Maybe this is what more looks like.

End of Play

NEW PLAYS

★ **YELLOW FACE by David Henry Hwang.** Asian-American playwright DHH leads a protest against the casting of Jonathan Pryce as the Eurasian pimp in the original Broadway production of *Miss Saigon*, condemning the practice as "yellowface." The lines between truth and fiction blur with hilarious and moving results in this unreliable memoir. "A pungent play of ideas with a big heart." —*Variety.* "Fabulously inventive." —*The New Yorker.* [5M, 2W] ISBN: 978-0-8222-2301-6

★ **33 VARIATIONS by Moisés Kaufmann.** A mother coming to terms with her daughter. A composer coming to terms with his genius. And, even though they're separated by 200 years, these two people share an obsession that might, even just for a moment, make time stand still. "A compellingly original and thoroughly watchable play for today." —*Talkin' Broadway.* [4M, 4W] ISBN: 978-0-8222-2392-4

★ **BOOM by Peter Sinn Nachtrieb.** A grad student's online personal ad lures a mysterious journalism student to his subterranean research lab. But when a major catastrophic event strikes the planet, their date takes on evolutionary significance and the fate of humanity hangs in the balance. "Darkly funny dialogue." —*NY Times.* "Literate, coarse, thoughtful, sweet, scabrously inappropriate." —*Washington City Paper.* [1M, 2W] ISBN: 978-0-8222-2370-2

★ **LOVE, LOSS AND WHAT I WORE by Nora Ephron and Delia Ephron, based on the book by Ilene Beckerman.** A play of monologues and ensemble pieces about women, clothes and memory covering all the important subjects—mothers, prom dresses, mothers, buying bras, mothers, hating purses and why we only wear black. "Funny, compelling." —*NY Times.* "So funny and so powerful." —*WowOwow.com.* [5W] ISBN: 978-0-8222-2355-9

★ **CIRCLE MIRROR TRANSFORMATION by Annie Baker.** When four lost New Englanders enrolled in Marty's community center drama class experiment with harmless games, hearts are quietly torn apart, and tiny wars of epic proportions are waged and won. "Absorbing, unblinking and sharply funny." —*NY Times.* [2M, 3W] ISBN: 978-0-8222-2445-7

★ **BROKE-OLOGY by Nathan Louis Jackson.** The King family has weathered the hardships of life and survived with their love for each other intact. But when two brothers are called home to take care of their father, they find themselves strangely at odds. "Engaging dialogue." —*TheaterMania.com.* "Assured, bighearted." —*Time Out.* [3M, 1W] ISBN: 978-0-8222-2428-0

DRAMATISTS PLAY SERVICE, INC.
440 Park Avenue South, New York, NY 10016 212-683-8960 Fax 212-213-1539
postmaster@dramatists.com   www.dramatists.com

NEW PLAYS

★ **A CIVIL WAR CHRISTMAS: AN AMERICAN MUSICAL CELEBRATION by Paula Vogel, music by Daryl Waters.** It's 1864 and Washington D.C. is settling down to the coldest Christmas Eve in years. Intertwining many lives, this musical shows us that the gladness of one's heart is the best gift of all. "Boldly inventive theater, warm and affecting." –*Talkin' Broadway.* "Crisp strokes of dialogue." –*NY Times.* [12M, 5W] ISBN: 978-0-8222-2361-0

★ **SPEECH & DEBATE by Stephen Karam.** Three teenage misfits in Salem, Oregon discover they are linked by a sex scandal that's rocked their town. "Savvy comedy." –*Variety.* "Hilarious, cliché-free, and immensely entertaining." –*NY Times.* "A strong, rangy play." –*NY Newsday.* [2M, 2W] ISBN: 978-0-8222-2286-6

★ **DIVIDING THE ESTATE by Horton Foote.** Matriarch Stella Gordon is determined not to divide her 100-year-old Texas estate, despite her family's declining wealth and the looming financial crisis. But her three children have another plan. "Goes for laughs and succeeds." –*NY Daily News.* "The theatrical equivalent of a page-turner." –*Bloomberg.com.* [4M, 9W] ISBN: 978-0-8222-2398-6

★ **WHY TORTURE IS WRONG, AND THE PEOPLE WHO LOVE THEM by Christopher Durang.** Christopher Durang turns political humor upside down with this raucous and provocative satire about America's growing homeland "insecurity." "A smashing new play." –*NY Observer.* "You may laugh yourself silly." –*Bloomberg News.* [4M, 3W] ISBN: 978-0-8222-2401-3

★ **FIFTY WORDS by Michael Weller.** While their nine-year-old son is away for the night on his first sleepover, Adam and Jan have an evening alone together, beginning a suspenseful nightlong roller-coaster ride of revelation, rancor, passion and humor. "Mr. Weller is a bold and productive dramatist." –*NY Times.* [1M, 1W] ISBN: 978-0-8222-2348-1

★ **BECKY'S NEW CAR by Steven Dietz.** Becky Foster is caught in middle age, middle management and a middling marriage—with no prospects for change on the horizon. Then one night a socially inept and grief-struck millionaire stumbles into the car dealership where Becky works. "Gently and consistently funny." –*Variety.* "Perfect blend of hilarious comedy and substantial weight." –*Broadway Hour.* [4M, 3W] ISBN: 978-0-8222-2393-1

DRAMATISTS PLAY SERVICE, INC.
440 Park Avenue South, New York, NY 10016 212-683-8960 Fax 212-213-1539
postmaster@dramatists.com   www.dramatists.com

NEW PLAYS

★ **AT HOME AT THE ZOO by Edward Albee.** Edward Albee delves deeper into his play THE ZOO STORY by adding a first act, HOMELIFE, which precedes Peter's fateful meeting with Jerry on a park bench in Central Park. "An essential and heartening experience." –*NY Times.* "Darkly comic and thrilling." –*Time Out.* "Genuinely fascinating." –*Journal News.* [2M, 1W] ISBN: 978-0-8222-2317-7

★ **PASSING STRANGE book and lyrics by Stew, music by Stew and Heidi Rodewald, created in collaboration with Annie Dorsen.** A daring musical about a young bohemian that takes you from black middle-class America to Amsterdam, Berlin and beyond on a journey towards personal and artistic authenticity. "Fresh, exuberant, bracingly inventive, bitingly funny, and full of heart." –*NY Times.* "The freshest musical in town!" –*Wall Street Journal.* "Excellent songs and a vulnerable heart." –*Variety.* [4M, 3W] ISBN: 978-0-8222-2400-6

★ **REASONS TO BE PRETTY by Neil LaBute.** Greg really, truly adores his girlfriend, Steph. Unfortunately, he also thinks she has a few physical imperfections, and when he mentions them, all hell breaks loose. "Tight, tense and emotionally true." –*Time Magazine.* "Lively and compulsively watchable." –*The Record.* [2M, 2W] ISBN: 978-0-8222-2394-8

★ **OPUS by Michael Hollinger.** With only a few days to rehearse a grueling Beethoven masterpiece, a world-class string quartet struggles to prepare their highest-profile performance ever—a televised ceremony at the White House. "Intimate, intense and profoundly moving." –*Time Out.* "Worthy of scores of bravissimos." –*BroadwayWorld.com.* [4M, 1W] ISBN: 978-0-8222-2363-4

★ **BECKY SHAW by Gina Gionfriddo.** When an evening calculated to bring happiness takes a dark turn, crisis and comedy ensue in this wickedly funny play that asks what we owe the people we love and the strangers who land on our doorstep. "As engrossing as it is ferociously funny." –*NY Times.* "Gionfriddo is some kind of genius." –*Variety.* [2M, 3W] ISBN: 978-0-8222-2402-0

★ **KICKING A DEAD HORSE by Sam Shepard.** Hobart Struther's horse has just dropped dead. In an eighty-minute monologue, he discusses what path brought him here in the first place, the fate of his marriage, his career, politics and eventually the nature of the universe. "Deeply instinctual and intuitive." –*NY Times.* "The brilliance is in the infinite reverberations Shepard extracts from his simple metaphor." –*TheaterMania.* [1M, 1W] ISBN: 978-0-8222-2336-8

DRAMATISTS PLAY SERVICE, INC.
440 Park Avenue South, New York, NY 10016 212-683-8960 Fax 212-213-1539
postmaster@dramatists.com www.dramatists.com

NEW PLAYS

★ **AUGUST: OSAGE COUNTY by Tracy Letts.** WINNER OF THE 2008 PULITZER PRIZE AND TONY AWARD. When the large Weston family reunites after Dad disappears, their Oklahoma homestead explodes in a maelstrom of repressed truths and unsettling secrets. "Fiercely funny and bitingly sad." *–NY Times.* "Ferociously entertaining." *–Variety.* "A hugely ambitious, highly combustible saga." *–NY Daily News.* [6M, 7W] ISBN: 978-0-8222-2300-9

★ **RUINED by Lynn Nottage.** WINNER OF THE 2009 PULITZER PRIZE. Set in a small mining town in Democratic Republic of Congo, RUINED is a haunting, probing work about the resilience of the human spirit during times of war. "A full-immersion drama of shocking complexity and moral ambiguity." *–Variety.* "Sincere, passionate, courageous." *–Chicago Tribune.* [8M, 4W] ISBN: 978-0-8222-2390-0

★ **GOD OF CARNAGE by Yasmina Reza, translated by Christopher Hampton.** WINNER OF THE 2009 TONY AWARD. A playground altercation between boys brings together their Brooklyn parents, leaving the couples in tatters as the rum flows and tensions explode. "Satisfyingly primitive entertainment." *–NY Times.* "Elegant, acerbic, entertainingly fueled on pure bile." *–Variety.* [2M, 2W] ISBN: 978-0-8222-2399-3

★ **THE SEAFARER by Conor McPherson.** Sharky has returned to Dublin to look after his irascible, aging brother. Old drinking buddies Ivan and Nicky are holed up at the house too, hoping to play some cards. But with the arrival of a stranger from the distant past, the stakes are raised ever higher. "Dark and enthralling Christmas fable." *–NY Times.* "A timeless classic." *–Hollywood Reporter.* [5M] ISBN: 978-0-8222-2284-2

★ **THE NEW CENTURY by Paul Rudnick.** When the playwright is Paul Rudnick, expectations are geared for a play both hilarious and smart, and this provocative and outrageous comedy is no exception. "The one-liners fly like rockets." *–NY Times.* "The funniest playwright around." *–Journal News.* [2M, 3W] ISBN: 978-0-8222-2315-3

★ **SHIPWRECKED! AN ENTERTAINMENT—THE AMAZING ADVENTURES OF LOUIS DE ROUGEMONT (AS TOLD BY HIMSELF) by Donald Margulies.** The amazing story of bravery, survival and celebrity that left nineteenth-century England spellbound. Dare to be whisked away. "A deft, literate narrative." *–LA Times.* "Springs to life like a theatrical pop-up book." *–NY Times.* [2M, 1W] ISBN: 978-0-8222-2341-2

DRAMATISTS PLAY SERVICE, INC.
440 Park Avenue South, New York, NY 10016 212-683-8960 Fax 212-213-1539
postmaster@dramatists.com www.dramatists.com